You Can Save Your Small Business

Who should read *You Can Save Your Small Business*?

You Can Save Your Small Business is a must for anyone struggling to keep a small business alive. It will also be very valuable to anyone who owns a small business, is thinking about starting a new business, or has been asked to invest in one.

Is your small business in trouble?

This book provides practical advice on what to do when you realize your small business is in trouble. Don't give up! You may still be able to turn your business around and make it thrive.

Thinking about starting a business?

Setting up a new business correctly is important to its ultimate success. *You Can Save Your Small Business* will provide you with many examples of how small businesses have been poorly set up and the consequences they suffered as a result. It will also suggest ways to start your business on a sound footing and operate it effectively.

Want to better understand the small business owner?

In this book Attorney William Manchee shares his insights acquired over the past forty-two years representing hundreds of small business owners in a myriad of situations as well as his own experiences in managing a small law firm. Learn valuable lessons through fictional accounts of actual business failures.

You Can Save Your Small Business

By
William Manchee, J.D.

Top Publications, Ltd.
Dallas, Texas

You Can Save Your Small Business

formerly *Yes, We're Open* and *Go Broke, Die Rich*

A Top Publications Library Edition

Third Edition

Top Publications, Ltd.

ISBN 1-7333283-2-7

The characters and events in this book are fictional and created out of the imagination of the author. Certain real locations and institutions are mentioned, but the characters and events depicted are entirely fictional.

Printed in the United States of America

Table of Contents

Be Free

America, land of the free.
But is that true for you and me?
Got to work to survive
In by nine, out by five

Can't be late, punch the clock
Work all day, shelves to stock
Shuffle paper here and there
Fold it, file it, mail it everywhere

Do this, do that. What'd you say?
Overtime? We have to stay?
Work, work, work, day and night
Got bills to pay, oh that's right

Tired of working, hate our plight?
Lets start a business, yes, that's right
Be independent, on our own
Not a greedy corporate drone

Come and go as we wish
Take a hike, catch some fish
No one cares, we're the boss
Lose a buck? That's our loss

Now we're free, free at last
Self-employed, what a blast
America, land of the free
At least that's so, for you and me

Introduction

Owning a successful small business is everyone's dream at one time or another. For only the self-employed are truly free. This revelation first came to me after I graduated from UCLA in the late '60s. After having struggled to get through college with a wife, two children, and another on the way, I was excited about the prospect of getting a job and finally starting to live the American dream.

After pouring through the classified ads in the *Dallas Morning News*, I made a list of interesting jobs that were available. There were quite a few, so I felt optimistic and started calling and lining up interviews. But when I started actually meeting with prospective employers, it wasn't long before an ominous feeling came over me. Most of my interviewers had somewhat of an arrogant attitude and showed me little respect. They weren't at all interested in selling me on the job, but only concerned with how I would fit into their operation. This was logical but also unsettling and made me realize that once I went to work for someone else, I would be under their thumb, forced to follow their rules, and accept what compensation they were willing to give me.

This gave me pause. Did I want my life and destiny in the hands of someone whose primary concern was their bottom line or personal profit? Could I trust an employer who promised me the stars to motivate me but would terminate me in a heartbeat the moment I no longer fit into their business plan? Was this the American dream I had worked so hard to achieve? I had heard about factory employees being laid off after years of service with little or no notice but hadn't given it much thought until then. Would this happen to me? Could I one day receive a pink slip instantly voiding years of hard work? Could I afford to give away this much control over my life? The answer was obviously no, so my job search came to an abrupt halt.

But if I couldn't work for someone else it seemed working for myself was my only option. The problem was I didn't have a business or profession to sustain me at the time, so much to my chagrin, I realized I needed to either start a business or go back to school and earn a professional degree. Having neither the cash, credit or knowledge to start a business, I opted to go to law school. I wasn't excited about going back to school. School had been difficult and tedious for me, but I realized I had no choice if I wanted to be truly free—free to carve out my own destiny in life and to achieve as much as my talents and ambitions would allow.

So, my wife and I struggled for three more years, both working while I went to SMU Law School. It was difficult, but we were confident our hard work and sacrifice would pay off in the end. After graduating and passing the bar, it took me over a year before I was able to hang out my shingle and start the practice of law. Fortunately, to support myself while in law school I sold insurance and made many friends in the insurance industry. I got involved in politics, too, which gave me the opportunity to meet many successful businessmen. So, it wasn't long before I was quite busy. Even so, being naive like most new entrepreneurs, I made many of the same mistakes I'll be warning you about later as we take a look at the perilous task of starting a new business.

Once becoming an entrepreneur myself, I became interested in helping other small business owners tackle the myriad of problems they faced every day. In time, it became my specialty of sorts, and over the years I have presided over the births and deaths of hundreds of small businesses. As an attorney, I have watched many of them grow, mature, and thrive, but I have seen many more stumble, fall, and die.

It is painful to see an entrepreneur, once so full of hope and excitement, suddenly desperate and defeated. I am saddened when I drive down the street and see an empty storefront, as I know someone has suffered an immeasurable loss and endured extraordinary grief and pain trying to save his piece of the American dream.

There are few experiences in life as painful and brutal as the failure of a small business. For a small business conceived and nurtured by its owner is like a living, breathing child. Its loss is no less traumatic than losing a loved one. After all, a business owner spends most of his waking hours at work. He will invariably become very attached to it, particularly if it is the business he loves and the one he has always wanted to pursue.

Inevitably the business becomes an extension of the owner himself. When it is ailing, he is ailing as well from stress and worry over whatever problems the business is facing. When the business is thriving, he will be happy, confident, and enjoying life to the fullest. If the business fails, the owner will feel like a failure and suffer deep emotional scars that will significantly impact his personal life for the rest of his life.

With business failure often comes marital strife and divorce. I don't claim to be a psychologist, but every day I see husbands and wives torn apart because one blames the other for a business failure. Or, if they don't blame each other, they are often so tired and battered from battling with creditors that they give up on the marriage. The sight of each other only brings back bad memories. Too often the unhappy couple opts for divorce. If the marriage does survive, it will never be the same.

Having watched my small business clients closely over the years and operating my own law practice, I have come to some conclusions about why some businesses succeed while others fail. The sad fact is that many of the businesses I have seen fail could have been successful had they been properly managed. The good news is that it's not too late for anyone still in business, even if they are only holding on by a thread. Once the entrepreneur realizes he is in trouble, there are a myriad of things that can be done to turn things around.

Don't get me wrong. This book doesn't contain any magical formula for success. Turning a business around requires hard work, discipline, and sacrifice. But what I hope this book will do is give the reader insight into why so many small businesses fail, allow them to identify their own shortcomings, and provide solutions and strategies that can help turn around an ailing business.

This book is intentionally written in a simple, informal style for the average business owner rather than for college graduates or MBAs. I've found that the cause of business failure isn't just a lack of education, experience, or business training, but just as often a lack of common sense. Often small business owners, or entrepreneurs, as I will call them from now on, do things they know are stupid and reckless. Why? Because entrepreneurs by definition are risk-takers. They like to experiment and do brash things that may only have a slim chance of success. They are the eternal optimist and often have unrealistic expectations.

Obviously, there are a lot of different kinds of small businesses, but for the purpose of this book that doesn't matter. I don't intend to dissect the workings of any particular type of business. I have found that most people who go into business know the basics of that particular enterprise. They have either worked for someone else in that field or have been trained somehow to perform their trade. What they usually are lacking is basic business training or experience.

The knowledge I have learned over the years has come primarily from trial and error rather than from a textbook or classroom instruction. Sometimes I've learned from my own mistakes, but more often it has been from the mistakes of my clients. Unfortunately, clients usually come to me after they are in trouble rather than consulting with me in the beginning, and possibly avoiding the problems that then confront them.

This book is not intended to be a manual or reference book. I hope that it will be interesting, entertaining, and informative. I fear too many self-help books get stuck on a shelf and never read cover-to-cover because they are too much like a textbook. This book is about adversity and how to overcome it. Its full of practical advice and ideas on how to deal with just about any adversity an entrepreneur might face.

Go Broke, Die Rich is full of real-life events that should be of interest to any entrepreneur. Obviously, the names and locations have been changed and the facts altered enough such that no confidences will be breached. Hopefully, you will be able to identify with the characters in these stories and understand the problems they face. If you are an entrepreneur, you will no doubt be facing similar issues and can learn from the mistakes made by the entrepreneurs in these stories.

As needed, I will explain some of the legal options available for the troubled small business, but these explanations will not be technical or hard to understand. It is not my intention to burden the reader with the complexities of the law, but simply to make him aware of available avenues for solving problems faced by entrepreneurs.

I consider every business failure a tragedy and, when it is one of my clients who goes down, it is even more troubling. I often lie awake at night wondering if there was something else I could have done to save a client's business and spare him and his family the dire consequences of a business failure. My only hope is that this book will help other entrepreneurs save their small businesses so they can live truly free and remain in control of their destiny.

Unfortunately, sometimes business failures are caused by larger forces that have nothing to do with how the business is being operated. These events and occurrences are usually unpredictable and may not be something that can be insured against. I don't know of any way to protect yourself against these larger forces that can overwhelm a small business owner at any time. The events of September 11, 2001, certainly couldn't have been anticipated or the economic meltdown of 2008. There is little a single entrepreneur can do when these cataclysmic events take place. Accordingly, I haven't dealt with that type of catastrophe in this book. My emphasis has been to concentrate on the more common issues, the avoidable pitfalls that every small business owner can protect himself against.

PART I - WHY BUSINESSES FAIL

1
Doomed from Day One

Many small businesses are doomed from day one—not because of the competition, undercapitalization, the economy, or a poor location, but because they think successfully operating a business is just a matter of hard work and dedication. From the moment they proudly frame their first dollar made and hang it on the wall, it is just a matter of time, days, weeks, or a few months before their business fails. When the doors open, they are full of excitement and hope, and expect only wonderful things to happen to them. Unfortunately, their destiny is already decided because they have no idea how to run a business.

I have a friend who is an amateur pilot. He loves flying and has a small plane that he meticulously maintains and flies on the weekends. He has logged hundreds of hours and I feel very comfortable flying with him. If anything were to go wrong, he would know what to do. I, on the other hand, know nothing about airplanes and if he were to have a heart attack while we were flying together, we would be in serious trouble. Sure, I've watched him fly the plane and it looks pretty easy, but the reality is that flying a plane is a very complicated and tricky business. Odds are I would crash the plane and we would both perish.

Many businesses look deceptively simple and

people think they will be easy to run. Rarely is that the case. Running a business without training and experience can be as tricky and dangerous as piloting an airplane for the very first time. Yet every day thousands of entrepreneurs embark on new business ventures with a vision but without any training or experience, with hope but without any realistic likelihood of success.

An excellent example was a client in the plumbing business, Roger Blake. He and his wife, Jane, had been running their small plumbing business for years. They did primarily subcontract work for home builders and had a good reputation. Jane handled the day-to-day operation of the business and Roger oversaw all the actual plumbing. Together they had been running the business well and making a good living.

Several years ago Roger called me in a panic and wanted to meet to discuss his deteriorating financial situation. That surprised me because they had always done so well in the past. When he came in he had a somber look on his face.

"So, you said over the telephone you were having some problems," I said.

Roger sighed. "Yes, the TEC. has locked me out of my business."

"What? How did that happen?" I asked.

I knew the Texas Employment Commission was very aggressive, usually much more so than the IRS, but it was unusual for a business to be completely shut down. That step was usually only taken if a taxpayer was totally uncooperative.

He shrugged. "I don't know. Jane usually took care of them. I guess I forgot to file the last two quarterly reports."

"Doesn't Jane handle that?" I asked.

"Ah. Well. Jane and I split up."

My heart sank. "Oh, no. How did that happen?"

"I don't know. When the kids grew up and left home we started growing apart. About three months ago she told me she was reevaluating her life and needed some time away to think."

"Oh, Jesus. I'm sorry. So, you've been running the business alone?"

"Right. My sister has been coming in to pay the bills but she doesn't know anything about taxes."

"Okay, so did you get the TEC reports filed?"

"No."

"Why not?"

"I sat down a couple times to do them, but it's hard to figure those forms out. I kept expecting Jane to come back and take care of it, but she didn't."

"So, how far behind our you?"

"They say $18,000 but that seems awfully high."

"That's because they have estimated your liability. You may not owe that much. They'll adjust it once you file your returns. Have you talked to them? They usually will let you work out an installment payment?"

"They won't let me do that until the reports are filed."

It suddenly occurred to me that if he wasn't filing TEC reports he probably wasn't filing his federal employment returns either.

"So, have you filed your 940 and 941s?" I asked.

He gave me a vacant stare.

Form 940 and 941 are employment tax returns

that every business must file if they have active employees. A separate employment tax return is usually filed with the state agency that deals with unemployment. In Texas it is the Texas Workforce Commission (formerly known as the Texas Employment Commission or TEC) who is responsible for handling unemployment insurance and claims.

"Okay," I laughed.

"Well, you've got three choices. You need to either reconcile with Jane, hire someone competent to replace her, or do what it takes to learn Jane's job and be prepared to work eighteen hours a day."

"Okay, I guess I'll get some help, but what about the lockout?"

"Give me TEC's contact information and I'll talk to them. If we file the delinquent returns quickly and propose a reasonable payment plan, they'll probably back off."

In Roger's case he knew the production and sales side of the business but was clueless when it came to the basics of running a small business. Roger wasn't happy having to take time away from sales and production, but he did hire a bookkeeper who got the returns filed for him. I then was able to get him on an installment payment plan with the TEC and he was back in business. Jane and Roger eventually got back together, but I still suggested he learn exactly what Jane did for the business in case for any reason she couldn't perform those functions in the future. It wasn't that I was pessimistic about his marriage, but I wanted him to appreciate his wife's important contribution to his success and to make him more appreciative of her hard work.

Then, if she ever left him again, got sick, or died, he would be able do her job, temporarily at least, until he could hire someone to take her place or find a new partner. Hopefully that wouldn't happen, but in a small business it was prudent to plan for every contingency.

In today's world opportunities abound for learning how to run a small business. The libraries and bookstores are full of books on the subject. Colleges and private institutions provide classes and training on almost every aspect of operating a business. The small business administration and other government agencies also have books, periodicals and training on these subjects. These educational and training opportunities require a time commitment, however, that many are not willing or able to give. Entrepreneurs starting a new business are usually anxious to get started and may not be willing to delay a month or two to get this basic business training. They figure they can learn on the job or hire someone to do these administrative tasks. Unfortunately, if the business gets off to a fast start, which is the goal of course, there won't be time to learn these basic skills and it won't be long before the business begins to suffer.

Experts will usually recommend that entrepreneurs develop a business plan before they go into business. This is sound advice and one of the first issues that should be addressed in a business plan is who will provide the basic administrative skills required to run the business. If the owner, one of the partners or shareholders don't have these requisite skills, or time to perform them, then they will have to be provided by an outside professional and the cost of those services will have to be figured into the business budget.

I'm not going to go into business plans in detail here. There are many articles, books, software programs or seminars on this topic that the entrepreneur can easily access. My point in bringing this up now is that within this first section of your business plan would be included topics such as handling of cash receipts, checking accounts, credit card processing, accounts receivable, accounts payable, financing, personnel, hours of operation, budgeting, telephones, computers, internet, advertising, and tax reporting and compliance. Each one of these topics are important and can become complicated so every entrepreneur should consider them carefully and develop an effective plan for dealing with them. And, of course, the business plan should be reduced to writing for later reference or for use to convince banks or investors to provide the necessary funds to operate the business.

Even if you develop a good business plan, that doesn't guarantee that your business will be successful. There are dozens of assumptions that will have to be made in order to build projections and models of the businesses' performance over the first few months or years. This will require considerable research on the entrepreneur's part or the input of persons experienced in the same or similar type businesses. Great care should be taken in making these assumptions. If any of them turn out to be wrong the consequences could be dire. When the business plan is finished you may realize your new enterprise won't work. If that happens, it will be tempting to go back and play with the numbers to make it work, but don't do it unless you are absolutely sure the changes you make are realistic. You will regret it later. On the other hand, don't let your business plan paralyze you.

I remember one of my clients coming to me with a business plan he and his partners had developed. It looked well thought out and quite feasible. I congratulated him and wished him well. A few weeks later the same client came back with a revised business plan with less optimistic expectations. It still looked good, so I commended him for being thorough and realistic. Months went by, however, and I hadn't heard anything, so I called the client and asked him how the new business was going.

"We haven't started it yet," he moaned.

"Why not?" I asked, quite surprised as I knew how anxious they were to get it going.

"I don't know. What if our cost assumptions are wrong? What if our sales projections don't materialize?"

I sighed. "Well, they probably will be wrong, but as long as you were careful in making them they should be reasonably close so that you can make adjustments elsewhere to compensate."

"I know, but the more we worked on the business plan the more things we thought of that could go wrong. I don't know if we should do this."

I laughed. "Listen, most of the clients I get in here don't even know what a business plan is. They started their businesses on a hope and a prayer. You have done your homework. You are prepared for every eventuality. Sure, you could still fail, the economy might crash tomorrow, but I think that's unlikely."

"Really? You think we're being paranoid?"

"Probably, but I can't guarantee your success. It's your decision. If you're not sure about it, don't do it."

A few weeks later they scrapped their business plan and all got jobs. I was disappointed but understood their decision. It takes a lot of courage to be an entrepreneur and risk everything for a dream. Not everyone is cut out for it. For me, I had no choice, I couldn't stand someone else controlling my life. When I was young both my parents worked very hard yet we still barely got by, so they didn't have time to micro manage my life. As long as I didn't get in trouble they left me alone. I got used to that and I liked the independence and freedom it allowed me. When I was drafted into the military in the late 60's I hated it because there I had no freedom whatsoever. Someone was always looking over my shoulder to make sure I was following every instruction and every rule to the letter. If I didn't, the consequences would be severe. So, every waking hour I went around with my stomach in a knot worried that I might unintentionally screw up somehow and get punished. When I got out of the military I vowed again to never be under someone's constant scrutiny again. So, self-employment was my only option.

But not everyone is like me. For those would-be entrepreneurs raised in a more controlled environment it might be a different story. If their parents micro-managed their lives, sent them to a boarding school or they served in the military, being on their own might be uncomfortable or even frightening.

When I was a teenager I had dreams of going into politics and running for office. I loved the excitement of campaigning, the political intrigue, the prestige of being an elected official, and the opportunity to make a difference in the world. While in high school I worked for a local congressman and enjoyed it immensely. So, after I graduated from high school and moved to Texas, I immediately got involved in the local political scene. It was fun at first and I got off to a decent start, but after a few years I realized I didn't have the charisma that a politician needed to get into national politics, nor was I willing to put politics ahead of my family which is another requirement to climb the political ladder. So, reluctantly, I gave up my childhood dream and decided to concentrate on my career and family. It was a painfully decision but prudent and necessary. Likewise, anyone who thinks they may want to start their own business needs to do some serious soul-searching to be sure that it is really what they want and they have the courage, drive and discipline to make it happen.

2
Looting

From my observation over the years, what I call "looting" is the primary reason small businesses fail. Looting results from the mistaken belief that the entrepreneur is owed a certain standard of living from the moment the new business is opened. Usually, the business plan will contain a budget projection to determine what compensation the business can support. Not that it is always possible to make a reliable projection, but it should at least be attempted with whatever information is available. Without this knowledge the entrepreneur either sets an arbitrary salary or takes money from the business as he needs it without regard to consequences of such action. Either way, if the salary is too high the business will start to slowly wither as the owner pockets precious operating capital until there isn't enough left to pay the bills as they come due.

Several years ago I represented a corporation that had been wholesaling gift items to retailers. There were four owners, all who were previously employed by a another very successful company in the same business. Over the years they came to realize that their hard work and skill was making their employer very rich. This realization caused them to ask for pay raises and better fringe benefits, which the owner refused to give them.

Bitter and frustrated over this lack of appreciation

for their value to the company they all decided they knew enough to quit and go into competition with their employer. Each of the four partners were well respected, knowledgeable in the trade, but none of them had ever operated a business before. Despite this handicap, their new enterprise flourished largely because they were able to lure away some very large customers from their previous employer.

Two years later when they came to see me, they were deeply in debt, owed substantial taxes to the IRS, and had been locked out by their landlord. As I was filling out a bankruptcy questionnaire, I asked them what compensation each was taking from the business. The CFO replied that each of the four stockholders had an annual salary of $150,000 and, of course, each was provided a Mercedes. When I quizzed them further, I found the new enterprise only had a half dozen other employees each earning less than $30,000 a year. This was less than a third of the number supporting their former company.

Common sense should have told them they didn't have a prayer of survival with this type of a cash flow drain, but each was used to a big salary and just assumed their new startup company could provide the same for them. What they should have done was not take a salary and split eighty percent of the profits between them each quarter. This might have been painful to them, but at least the business would have had a chance of survival.

This is an extreme example of looting. Usually it is less obvious. For example, one of my first clients was a fine tailor from Italy, Gino Ricardo and his wife Victoria.

He was always very busy, often working ten or twelve hours a day. Operating as a sole proprietor, he had only one checking account from which he paid all his personal and business expenses. Being good Catholics, they had many children, and as their kids got older, household expenses rose dramatically. Soon the business started to have cash flow problems. The rent was late, tax deposits were missed, the electric company was threatening to cut off the power, and checks were bouncing. That's when Gino and his wife came to see me.

"So, you said something about electricity getting cut off?" I said to break the ice.

Victoria nodded. She managed the business as her husband barely spoke English. "Yes, unless we pay them $2,582 by 5:00 p.m. on Friday they are going to cut it off."

"So is there any way you can find that kind of money?" I asked, already knowing the answer.

She shook her head. "No, we went to the bank but they won't help us because we're late on our line of credit."

That didn't surprise me as banks were not usually much help once you got in trouble. At that point all a bank was usually concerned about was how you were going to pay them what you owed.

It was painful to see Gino and Victoria in this situation as I had known them for several years. I met them while selling life insurance when I was in law school. I sold Gino my very first life insurance policy a week after I went to work for Metropolitan Life. Three years later when I hung up my shingle, they were there to have me draw up a will. They were very nice people and

I was very fond of them.

The first thing I do when a client with financial problems comes to see me is create a budget. It only takes an hour or two and the cause of the problem often becomes apparent when the process is complete. Sadly, for most of these clients it's the first time they have ever done a budget. When I start asking questions about their income and expenses, they usually put up a fight complaining that they don't have all the information they need, or they need their bookkeeper or accountant to help them. But I don't let them off the hook, because if I leave it to them it will rarely get done.

So, I assure them that all the information I will need they will be able to provide me off the top of their head. They usually give me a skeptical look but I just smile and start asking questions. I think the reason my clients are so resistant to doing a budget is twofold. First, they think it is more complicated than it is, and secondly, they are afraid of what the budget will reveal.

Many small business owners, if not most, do their bookkeeping in their heads. They know, or think they know, from day to day where they stand both financially and operationally. Unfortunately, as the business gets more and more complicated these mental impressions are often false.

I tell my clients a budget is really quite simple. All they need to give me is an estimate of what revenue they have coming in each month and what expenses they expect to incur. As I pull up a simple spreadsheet on my computer, I start throwing out categories like sales receipts, advertising expense, travel, maintenance, and then record their answers. If they shrug and claim not to know, I make them give me a guesstimate which they can later verify. When the spreadsheet is printed out, it will usually reveal that their monthly cash outflow far exceeds their monthly receipts. This often shocks them, but just as often they just nod like they knew this all along.

Gino shrugged when I told him his expenses exceeded his income by nearly a thousand dollars a month.

"We're not spending money on anything frivolous," Victoria assured me. "In fact, I haven't bought a new dress or a pair of shoes in two years."

"I know, but that's not the point. If the business only has a profit of one thousand dollars and you take out two thousand the business has lost a thousand dollars. Pretty soon that ads up and eventually the business can't pay all its bills in a timely manner."

Gino leaned forward. "But Mr. Manchee, I had two customers who owed me lots of money. They promised to pay so I pay myself what I need thinking they will honor their word."

"I know. But you can't do that. You need to wait until they actually write you a check and it clears the bank."

Gino sighed and shook his head. "Those dirty bastards!'

I laughed. "I know. Customers who are slow pays are a big problem, so you have to consider what they owe you as a bad debt until they actually come through with the cash."

In his heart Gino knew that I was right, but hadn't been able to face reality. It's just human nature to want to believe someone when they make a promise to you. For this reason you should always try to get your customers to pay cash and leave the lending to the banks and credit card companies. Even without Gino collecting his delinquent receivables he figured business would improve and eventually his income would catch up with his expenses. This was extremely unrealistic but a common belief among entrepreneurs.

"So, what are we supposed to do if we need three thousand a month but the business only has two thousand dollars profit," Victoria said obviously frustrated.

"Well, you either cut your personal expenses or one of you get a part time job to supplement your income until the business can support the income you need."

Victoria took a deep breath and shook her head in despair.

"Had you come to me sooner, before you got so far in the hole, we could have figured out your problem sooner and maybe avoided this cash flow problem."

Victoria and Gino just looked at me guiltily. I knew one of the reasons they had waited so long to come see me was due to the fact they knew they'd have to pay for my services and attorneys weren't cheap. Only when the situation got critical did they give me a call. This was not only a problem for them but for me as well. With money in short supply, paying an attorney is no easy trick. Gino offered me a custom suit in exchange for my help. It was the last thing I needed, but I couldn't let down my very first client.

We wanted to set up a payment plan with the utility company but they weren't interested, so I had to put Gino and Victoria in Chapter 13 to protect them from a power outage and the wrath of their other creditors who were after them. This worked out well and, after three tough years, Gino paid off all his creditors and life got back to normal. Gino and his family had survived and I was looking good in my custom-made Italian suit.

Even when I was able to get a client to acknowledge that he was looting his company, it wasn't always easy to get them to stop. I can testify to this as I was guilty of looting my own law practice for many years. We were simply living above our means and the only source of revenue was the practice. I took what was needed to pay my personal bills, and there was nobody to tell me to stop.

The dire consequences of looting are often postponed by excessive borrowing. When the business starts to run low on cash the natural thing to do is to borrow money. Unfortunately, this only makes matters worse as interest expense is added to the already overburdened budget, and eventually the borrowed money has to be repaid. Since bankers don't usually lend money to a business without collateral, the entrepreneur now must pledge all his personal assets and personally guarantee this new indebtedness.

The only way out of this inevitable path to doom is extraordinary sales, unexpected windfalls, or wealthy relatives–none which are a safe bet. Even if the entrepreneur is a great salesman, a scientific genius, or on the cutting edge of his profession, the lack of fundamental business acumen will eventually catch up with him.

This was the case with a computer genius, Sam Sturgeon. He had invented one of the first personal computers back in the eighties and had received a lot of good press. Sam, too, had made his employer very rich and he decided he wanted some of that wealth for himself. With the profits he'd socked away he opened up a new computer manufacturing company. His new line of computers were state-of-the-art and sold like snow cones on a hot Sunday afternoon when they first came out. He had a nice manufacturing plant in northwest Dallas with about twenty-five employees and his future looked bright.

Six months later Sam called up and said he need to see me about a Chapter 11. This is another form of bankruptcy utilized normally by corporations, partnerships or large sole proprietorships who want to stay in business but need to reorganize their affairs. I was flabbergasted as he had previously hired me to develop an elaborate estate plan to protect the millions he'd made in the computer business.

"So, what's going on?" I asked him. "I thought you were set for life."

"Yeah, well I'm on the verge of a breakthrough but I need a little more time."

"Well, that's one of the nice things about Chapter 11. It will buy you at least four to six months."

"Really? How's that?"

"Well. Under Chapter 11 you can't legally pay your unsecured debt until your plan is confirmed and that takes about four to six months. Then, whatever unsecured debt you end up paying can be spread out over a period of five years or more."

"What about the loans to the bank?"

"You'll still have to deal with the banks. How is your relationship with them?"

Sam shrugged. "They're not so happy with me right now."

"How far behind are you?"

"Well, I'm not behind. I've made all my interest payments but they've been wanting me to pay down the principle."

"So, what about all the money you made when you sold your patent?"

"It's pretty much gone," Sam confessed.

I was afraid to ask where it had gone but I needed to know. "So, what happened to it?"

"Well, I've always been a NASCAR fan."

A sick feeling came over me. "Don't tell me you're sponsoring a NASCAR racing team."

He nodded. "Are you a racing fan? One of our mechanics is in the back working on the car right now. You want to see it?"

I laughed. "Sure, why not. I've never seen one before up close."

He led me back through the manufacturing plant. It was a very impressive operation except that it appeared to be shut down.

"So, where is everybody?"

"Oh, I sent everybody home. We're out of parts and there is no use having them sitting around doing nothing."

"Right," I agreed.

When we got back to the garage I saw a mechanic working on an engine. An attractive blond woman in blue jeans and a Dallas Cowboy T-Shirt was watching him work. Sam introduced me to the mechanic, Warren Rogers and his girlfriend, Gwen. I wondered how much a mechanic for an Indy racing team was paid but I was afraid to ask.

"This is a Dodge, 750 horsepower, 358 cubic inch engine," Sam advised. "Pretty sweet, huh?"

"For sure," I said amazed at how big the engine was. "So, when is your next race?"

Sam shrugged. "I don't know. It depends on how long it takes Warren to get this car rebuilt. Our driver got caught in the middle of a bad accident in his last race and nearly destroyed this baby. He was lucky he got out alive."

"Oh, no. Is he okay?"

"He is now after two surgeries and a hundred grand out of pocket."

"You didn't have insurance?"

Sam shook his head. "No. Too expensive. I'm just hoping he doesn't sue. I don't have workmen's comp."

Sam story was getting worse by the minute. I couldn't wait to hear the rest of the saga. When he finally laid it out for me all I could do was cringe at his stupidity. He'd developed a state of the art point-of-sale computer system and had already pre-sold it to several cruise lines. Unfortunately, because he'd blown most of his capital on the racing team he was forced to borrow the money to fund his research and development. Unfortunately, it took him longer to work the kinks out of the system than he had expected and his bankers got spooked and called the note. Without capital or income he got behind on his rent and was about to get locked out of his manufacturing facility.

After shutting down Sam's racing operation, we put his company in Chapter 11 and tried to reorganize. It was difficult case because he had waited too long to file and had virtually no cash. We did finally get his Chapter 11 confirmed, but while he was distracted by the bankruptcy, his competitors overtook him technologically and he was never able to get back on top. Eventually he had to shut down and convert to Chapter 7. He had lost everything.

It's not uncommon for someone who struggles for success and finally achieves it to think the battle is over and let down his guard. But the truth is, it's often harder to keep money than it is to earn it in the first place. The temptation to spend money sitting in a bank account or to let someone else spend it for you, is often so intense that only getting rid of it will once again bring peace.

A professional athlete was referred to me many years ago. He had come from a poor family and had been a neighborhood hero throughout high school and college. When he made it big in NBA his family and friends decided he should open up a chain of restaurants. I was excited about seeing him because of his notoriety, but I was also anxious to help him get his business venture off to a good start.

Unfortunately, when he came in he was accompanied by his mother and several close friends. They were treating him like he was some kind of god and made it virtually impossible for me to talk candidly with him. As the meeting progressed, he told me of several loans to friends he was thinking about making and several joint ventures he was in the process of negotiating. Although he had a nice salary, he had no other assets. I cautioned him to take it slow and not get involved in a bunch of ventures he knew nothing about. His mother and friends became indignant and, needless to say, my services were quickly terminated.

A year or two later his career started going downhill and it wasn't long before he was out of the NBA. Although I don't know for sure, I suspect he has nothing left of the millions he received while playing professional basketball.

The point is, smart and talented business owners need to have a sound game plan just as much as the average ones. Brains and talent may prolong the date of business failure, but they won't prevent it.

The only way to stop looting a business is to set a modest, realistic salary that the business can easily support. Then at the end of the year, if there has been a profit and there is extra cash in the bank, the owner can take a bonus at that time. Conversely, if the business is still losing money, then the salary is too high and should be cut. This isn't to say that the business owner can't do other things to increase revenue or cut expenses, but until a profit is realized and there is extra cash in the bank, no bonuses should be declared.

The problem with looting is it's not a business issue, but a problem at home. The failure of an entrepreneur to get on top of his own personal budget can destroy his chances of successfully owning and operating a business. The situation is further complicated if the spouse isn't a part of the business and doesn't appreciate the fact that the family must live on the profits of the business rather than a set salary. If the owner has trouble grasping this reality you can imagine how hard it is for a spouse who is often charged with administering the family budget. How can you run a household when you don't know how much your income will be each month? The answer is simple but not easy to swallow. The owners or partners are paid a very modest salary that the business can easily sustain, and if there are actual profits they can be split periodically, usually quarterly or less frequently.

Unfortunately, determining the amount of profits that can be safely distributed is no easy task if income is not uniform and steady. For instance in my own situation where our law firm works on a contingent fee basis and only gets paid when a case is settled or collected at trial, there can be months that go by without any revenue whatsoever. So, when cash does finally come in it must be carefully allocated first to the payment of outstanding bills, then to expenses that will be incurred before the next money is expected and, if anything is left over, split as profit to the owners. As you can imagine, if it has been a while since an owner or partner has been paid anything over and above his modest salary, they are going to be very anxious for a distribution. If there isn't anything left to distribute, the partners or the business owners' spouses may be quite upset. Sometimes they are so upset with this reality that it affects their performance and puts the company's very survival at risk.

For many businesses income won't fluctuate so radically as in my example, but there will invariably be ups and downs in any business, so the entrepreneur, his partners and their spouses must realize this and be prepared for it. If this is the case, like I said before, difficult decisions will have to be made. Perhaps the owner's spouse will have to get a job or their lifestyle will have to be curtailed until the business is built up and can support a larger salary. The entrepreneur must be strong in this regard and avoid the temptation to loot the company or run up personal credit card debt to offset this lack of income. If this can't be done, then the sensible thing for the entrepreneur to do is shut down the business and go work for someone else .

3
Suffocation

In the euphoria of starting a new business, the temptation is to go first class no matter what the entrepreneur's financial situation might be. Unfortunately, first class is expensive. Often two or three times more than what is actually needed. Few newly formed businesses can afford this excess overhead. At the start of any new business, cash is almost always a precious commodity and should be carefully watched and controlled. Because of this reality, initial overhead should be kept to a minimum. If it is too high the business will be in distress from day one.

It's often said that the success of a business depends on three things: location, location, and location. Too often the new business owner is obsessed with this principal and opens up in a prime location neither he nor the business can afford. Typically he will lease this real estate in a strip center or shopping mall for a three to five-year period at an astronomical rent that even a seasoned business would have trouble supporting. By the time the business is up and running it is already in crisis. Each month cash flow is a major problem distracting the owner from the critical needs of the new enterprise.

I remember Paul Blazer a very bright entrepreneur who designed computer chips. For years he had a lucrative contract with TI, employed several other engineers, and was doing quite well. Then, the semi conductor industry took a nosedive, his contract wasn't renewed, and there seemed to be little hope that he could get a new contract. Frustrated and depressed, he started looking for a new business and came to me to talk about it.

"So, there's no hope for you design business?" I asked.

He sighed. "No. I'm afraid not. I've contacted a dozen other companies and everybody is cutting back. They're doing everything in-house until the market turns around."

"So, what are you going to do?"

"Well, a friend of mine wants to start a restaurant."

"A restaurant?"

"Yeah. He's got a new concept—salads."

"Salads?"

"Yes, we're going to call it "Just Salads." You know how everyone is so health conscious—particularly women."

"Don't you think you'll be limiting your customer base too much just serving salads. I'd never eat at your restaurant. I rarely eat salads and I think a lot of guys are like that."

"I don't think so. We've read market studies and the demand for salads has been increasing dramatically every year. We figure, if we offer an extensive variety of salads unavailable anywhere else, that customers will flock to us."

Paul's argument sounded good but I wasn't convinced he'd get enough traffic to survive. It wasn't my place, however, to tell him what to do with his life, so I expressed my misgivings and then turned to more practical concerns.

"Okay. So, let's say you do attract the customers you hope to, what do you and your partner know about running a restaurant. Do either of you have any experience in restaurant operations?"

"No, but we both like to cook and I've run my design business for over ten years."

I laughed. "I know the restaurant business might seem fairly straight forward, but let me assure you it's one of the most difficult businesses to operate and sustain for any length of time. I've put more restaurants through bankruptcy than you can imagine."

Paul shrugged. "We know it will be hard work but we feel good about it. We just need you to set us up a corporation and look over the lease we're negotiating."

When he brought a proposed lease to me, I gasped at the huge base rental. The lease also provided for the payment of a percentage of revenue in addition to the base monthly rental.

"This rent is a little steep don't you think?" I said.

"Yeah, but this a great location. Right downtown in the financial district. The lunch business will be out of sight."

"But you won't have much dinner traffic, will you?"

"You'd be surprised how many people eat downtown after work."

"How do you know that?"

"Well, I've been hanging around downtown a lot and watching where people are going at lunch and after work. The restaurants in the area seem pretty busy at night."

I was skeptical but there wasn't much I could do as Paul had obviously already made up his mind. "This lease has a percentage rental clause?" I pointed out.

"What's that?"

"That means on top of the base rent they want a percentage of your profits."

"Oh. Right. The landlord said that was standard downtown."

"I don't think so. I'd scratch out that clause. You're rent is already too high."

"But he said he wouldn't lease us the spot without that clause."

"I'm sure he did, but I'm sure he doesn't want the property vacant either. You've got to negotiate. Don't act like you've got to have this location. I'd ask him to come down on the base rent too. You're going to have trouble making a profit if you don't."

"But our realtor says there are two other people looking at the space. We don't want to lose out on this location."

"You should keep looking. I'm sure you can find a less expensive spot that is just as good."

"No. We've already looked. This is the only location that is suitable for what we want to do."

Fortunately, it's not an attorney's job to be a mother. Sometimes I had to let my clients make a mistake, even if I knew in my heart it was a big one. Nevertheless, this was one of such magnitude that I persisted in objecting to the cost of the lease and almost got fired. When the restaurant opened to much fanfare, I held my breath.

Needless to say, the restaurant didn't last six months, but it wasn't because the concept wasn't good. In fact, salad restaurants popped up all over the Metroplex soon after my client's enterprise hit the bankruptcy court. From day one the overhead had been so high the restaurant had no chance of success.

In order for the typical under-capitalized small business to survive, overhead must be kept very modest such that a profit can still be made even when times are slow. This is why there are so many small, successful family run businesses opened up by new immigrants. Labor being the most expensive operating expense, they have an advantage because the family members perform most, if not all, of the labor for the business. These family members don't have to get a regular paycheck and often work for food, lodging, and a little spending money while they go to school or look for outside employment.

I recall getting a call once from a man who had opened a Chinese restaurant, Don Chan. It was in a strip shopping center in a growing suburb of Dallas. It was his second restaurant but, unlike his first, he was compelled to staff the new restaurant with outside personnel since his family had its hands full with the first restaurant. Although business was okay, he had fallen behind on the rent and the landlord was threatening to lock him out. When Don came in and we looked at his finances more closely, I realized his business could never be successful because the rent and labor costs were too high. Even if we had filed a Chapter 11 it most likely wouldn't have been successful because the business couldn't make a profit given the rent and labor costs. He finally filed Chapter 7 and moved on.

Several months later I noticed that a Mexican restaurant had opened up in the same space in the shopping center. At the time I thought it was a very dangerous move since obviously this was a bad location for a restaurant. Curious about the new business, I had dinner there with my wife one night and introduced myself to the proud owner. In our conversation he acknowledged that most everyone working in the restaurant was family. The husband ran the wait staff, the wife did the cash register and some aunts and uncles handled the cooking. In addition, since the previous restaurant had gone under, the landlord was forced to reduce the rent to attract a new tenant. The reduction in rent and having much of the labor handled by family members was a significant factor in the new venture's success. Ten years later we still eat at this restaurant at least once a week, and it just goes to show you that location isn't the only factor to consider in starting a new business. Overhead is just as important.

This also illustrates the importance of researching the competition. As part of his business plan, the entrepreneur should study the competition in his sales area and see if any of them have a unique advantage that will make competition difficult. Besides employing family members to cut labor costs, the competition may be a franchise business which will have the advantage of an established business name, enhanced advertising and franchise training for the owner and personnel. If the competition is not part of a franchise, it may well be one of several locations of a business owned by an individual or corporation that will provide financial support. In fact, often times when a second or third location is opened up it is expected to operate at loss for a period of time and the owner is prepared to cover that loss. Should an entrepreneur find himself in competition with a subsidized location it may greatly diminish any chance of success.

The entrepreneur should also be prudent in equipping his new business. Everything in a business doesn't have to be state of the art and brand new. Functionality is what is important. Many times I have seen entrepreneurs purchase or lease expensive computer networks, classy furniture, elaborate phone systems, and other things that aren't absolutely necessary for the business to be successful. I remember one particular situation that was particularly egregious. An attorney friend, who I will call Dan, came to me after he was sued by the leasing company that had funded the copiers he had purchased for his new title company. When I read the lawsuit I was shocked to find out he had leased seven high volume copiers with a total lease expense of nearly $3,000 per month. The leases were for three years which meant he would be paying $108,000 and not ever own the copiers at the end of the lease. When Dan came in I asked him about it.

"So, why do you need seven copiers?" I asked.

"Do you know how much paper is involved in a real estate closing?"

"Sure, a lot, but how many closings do you do in a day?"

"I don't know, several."

"How many closers do you have?"

"Two and myself," Dan replied. "And they each have a secretary."

"So, wouldn't three copiers be enough?"

"When we are closing a case we can't be standing around waiting for a copier to be freed up. Time is money."

"Still, that's $3,000 a month and you obviously can't afford it?"

"Well, we charge for copies."

"Okay, so why didn't you pay the lease payments then."

Dan shrugged.

Dan had obviously gone overboard on copiers but he wouldn't admit it. Plus, leasing equipment is expensive. It's much cheaper to buy equipment and finance it over as short a period as possible. Needless to say, Dan's title company didn't last long. His copier problems were just the tip of the iceberg and it wasn't long before his title underwriters shut him down.

4
Starting on a Shoe String

As mentioned earlier, under-capitalization is a major cause of small business failure, particularly with so many chain stores and franchise operations muscling their way into almost every neighborhood. For some service businesses like a law office, insurance agency, realtor, or accounting firm, capital isn't as critical as it is in other businesses. Some businesses, such as printers, manufacturers, wholesalers, retailers, or auto repair shops require extensive furniture, equipment and inventory. For the later, starting with adequate capitalization is critical for their survival.

A few years back, I had two clients in the wholesale distribution business who were both quite successful—JB Gift Distributors and Addison Electric. But their success came only after very painful business failures largely due to inadequate capitalization. Both owners had learned their trade while working for other similar companies. After a while, they believed they had the expertise to run their own companies, so they ventured out on their own. Lacking capital, they borrowed heavily to purchase the bare minimum inventories and supplies they needed to start their businesses. Their hope was to reinvest profits to buy inventory over the first year or two of operations. Unfortunately, this was the mid-80s just before Black Monday when the economy collapsed and many banks and savings and loans went under.

Sales immediately fell and profits dried up. With no cash reserves, their inventories quickly shrank as they were not able to replace what was sold or used up. In a matter of weeks they found themselves behind on their office leases, in default on their lines of credit, and struggling to meet payroll and pay IRS withholding.

When a business is on the brink of failure there are only a few options. The first is to invest sufficient money into the business so it can continue to operate and hope you can figure out how to turn things around. The second is to reorganize under Chapter 11 or Chapter 13 of the United States Bankruptcy Code. Chapter 13 is for individuals with debts below a certain maximum and Chapter 11 is for individuals whose debts exceed that maximum or businesses that are organized as corporations, partnerships or limited liability companies. The third option when the situation is dire is to cease operations and file Chapter 7.

Neither company was able to find additional capital, so they ended up in bankruptcy, one in Chapter 7 and the other in Chapter 11.

JB stood for Jim Burrows, a fantastic salesman but a man who was horrible with paperwork, budgeting and finance. Believing somehow the economy would miraculously turn around, he delayed coming to see me until his situation was desperate. As soon as he got to my office he handed me a citation he had just been served.

"So, who's suing you?" I asked.

"One of my suppliers. He put me on COD a year

ago but here recently demanded I pay the old balance. I guess he's hurting too."

"How much is it?"

"Eighty-two grand. If I tried to pay him everything I owed, I wouldn't have any capital to run the business."

"If he cuts you off, can you find a new supplier?" I asked.

"Sure, there are other vendors out there but he's the most competitive?"

"Do you have any secured creditors like banks or leasing companies?"

"No. Just a lot of vendors and the IRS."

"Well, it sounds like you need to file a Chapter 11. That way you will be able to eliminate fifty to eighty percent of you unsecured debt and payout IRS over five or six years."

"Really, I can do that?"

"Probably. The creditors have to approve your plan but they usually will vote for it if you give them a significant dividend. They know if they don't approve it you'll file a Chapter 7 and they'll get nothing."

"What kind of dividend?"

"Usually ten to twenty-five percent is enough."

"So, I can write off 75% of my debts?"

"Un huh."

"So, what's the downside?"

"Well. The only complication is the creditor's committee, if one is appointed. If so, we'll have to negotiate with them to get your plan approved."

"What's your fee going to be?"

"It depends but if we don't have any major fights it shouldn't be more than $10-15,000."

Jim gasped. "That much?"

"Yes, I'm afraid so, but you'll be paying it out over a year to eighteen month period so it won't be so bad."

Jim laughed. "That's easy for you to say."

Jim decided to go ahead with the Chapter 11 and it worked well for him. The creditors committee opposed nearly everything we did, but eventually they realized that getting something was better than nothing. We settled by agreeing to pay twenty-five cents on the dollar rather than the ten percent we initially had proposed. By the next summer JB's plan was confirmed and the business came out of bankruptcy stronger than ever. After shedding seventy-five percent of its debt and being allowed to pay out IRS over six years, the business thrived.

Addison Electric wasn't so lucky. Ronnie Clark came in one afternoon looking tired and depressed.

"So, over the phone you mentioned you were having problems with your bank?"

"Yes, the bastards called my note and now they're suing me."

"Why?"

Ronnie shook his head. "Business has been a little slow so I haven't been able to make any principal reductions on my line of credit. I've paid the interest as it came due, but I just haven't had any extra money to pay down the loan."

"What kind of collateral do they have?" I asked.

"Collateral?"

"Yeah. Usually when a bank loans you money they require a blanket security interest on all of your assets."

"Really? They didn't mention it."

"I'm sure they did but you were probably so

anxious to get the loan you didn't pay attention to what they were saying. You should have brought me the loan documents to look over. I would have made sure you understood what you were signing."

"It wouldn't have made any difference," Ronnie replied. "I needed the money, so I probably would have signed whatever they put in front of me."

That was probably true. Most people who borrowed money accepted whatever terms were offered by the lender without question. They didn't realize that the terms of a loan were often negotiable and a little haggling could get them less onerous terms.

I started reading the petition that had been served on Jim and they were, in fact, claiming a security interest on all of his assets including the cash in the bank, accounts receivable, equipment and general intangibles."

"So, what does that mean?" Jim asked.

"Well, it means you can't touch your cash, collect your receivables, or sell your equipment.

"What! How can I do business if can't use my cash or collect my receivable?"

"You can't unless you file a Chapter 11 reorganization."

"Bankruptcy?" Jim asked.

"Yes, I'm afraid so. The problem is once you file you'll have to get the bank's agreement to use your cash collateral."

"What does that mean?"

"It means we'll have to sit down with the bank and get them to agree to let you use your cash and receivables to continue in business."

"But it's my cash and my receivables," Ronnie

protested.

"Sure, but they have a security interest in it so they have the right to keep you from impairing their collateral. How is your relationship with the bank been?"

"Obviously, not so great if they are suing me."

"Well, do you know any of the bank officers very well?"

"No. Not really. The loan officer I initially got the loan with has long since moved on to another bank. I really don't know anyone over there anymore."

"Hmm. Well, we should probably talk to the bank before you file and see if we have any chance of cutting a deal. If the bank doesn't want to cooperate, it will make getting a plan approved difficult and expensive."

"Wonderful."

"There's another option you could consider," I said.

"What's that?"

"You could just shut down the business, file a chapter 7 bankruptcy and then down the road after the dust settles you could start a new business."

"Won't I lose everything in the Chapter 7?"

"Yes, the bank will take all its collateral, so you'll have to start from scratch but it should be a lot easier the second time around. Your best bet is to find an investor who will put up the money to get started without an expectation of being paid back right away. Of course, he'll get a portion of the profits but you won't actually have to pay him unless there is a profit."

"Really. That's sounds great, but where do I find an investor?"

"I can't help you with that, but I bet if put your mind to it you can come up with some prospects. Before you talk to them, though, you need to have a business plan put together so you can show them their investment will pay off."

"How do I do a business plan?"

"There are books and computer software available that will take you step by step through the process of doing a business plan. Since you know the business already it probably won't be very hard for you to answer all the questions and fill in the blanks. It will be a good exercise anyway since it will force you to do a budget."

"Won't I get in trouble if I shut down my business and then start it up again in a few months?"

"Not if you set up a brand new company and get new funding. You'll have to turn over all the assets of the old company to your trustee to liquidate. You can't hold anything back. If you want any of the assets of the old business you can bid on them when the trustee puts them up for sale."

"What about my customers?"

"You wouldn't be able to solicit old customers since your customer list is an asset of the estate, however, if the trustee doesn't sell the list and closes out the estate, then they would be fair game."

"That may be the way to go then."

"I think so. If you file a Chapter 11 you'll have to pay most of your secured debt and that could prove difficult."

Ronnie finally decided Chapter 7 was the only feasible way to rid himself of the bank loan and the vendor debt that had gotten out of hand. Although he would have preferred to pay his creditors that wasn't really an option in the current business climate. So,

Ronnie started over but he waited until he'd lined up a couple of investors to put up the necessary capital for the new venture. Armed with the knowledge learned from his first entry into the small business arena he avoided his past mistakes and soon had a flourishing business.

Before long Ronnie was coming to see me for estate and tax planning rather than dealing with angry creditors. His business grew rapidly over the next few years and now is worth millions. But he was only able to launch his new business because he had a client base established. He was lucky in this regard, because an astute Chapter 7 trustee would have recognized the value of the client base and tried to sell it rather than ignoring it and closing out the case. Fortunately for him, most Chapter 7 trustees are so busy and overburdened that they rarely go after an intangible asset like goodwill. They tend to focus on hard assets like vehicles, inventory, equipment, and accounts receivable. In this case, the trustee never even considered the most valuable asset of all, a list of over five hundred active clients who ordered electrical parts and supplies almost every week.

So why do entrepreneurs start a business when they know that they don't have enough capital? Is it overconfidence, unrealistic optimism, or stupidity? My observation is that it is all of the above, plus a denial of reality. Some people, like myself, believe they have no choice. They are convinced they would be miserable if they worked for someone else. Others see it as the only way to have a chance at becoming rich and famous. Why work to make someone else wealthy, I often hear them say. Others have great dreams and aspirations that they feel will never be obtained if someone else controls their destiny. These entrepreneurs often become obsessed with making their dreams a reality, so much so that they often overlook or ignore the obvious risks and pitfalls that lay before them. They simply don't care about reality. In their minds somehow they will overcome the odds and achieve success. It's a tragic case of self-deception. So many entrepreneurs start off their new businesses keenly aware that they are grossly under-capitalized, but believing firmly, nevertheless, that somehow they will survive and be successful.

5
Giving it Away

Another big cause of small business failure, particularly in the construction industry, is bidding the job so low that there is no way a profit could possibly be made. This usually occurs when there is competition for the job and the small business owner desperately needs the work. It's a very common practice in the construction business to borrow from Peter to pay Paul, as the saying goes. It works like this.

The owner bids the job too low and then runs out of money to complete it. Rather than default on the project, get sued, and be put out of business, he runs out and gets another job. With the up-front money on the new job, he completes the old one. This will work for a while, but eventually the contractor either won't be able to get a new job quickly enough, or the up-front money he gets on the second job isn't sufficient to finish the first job.

This is when I usually get the phone calls and confessions from my construction clients that they have underbid a job and can't finish it. Before they call me, they have usually exhausted any possibility of getting a new job or borrowing the money. By this time the customer is belligerent and may have contacted an attorney. This is when I usually suggest Chapter 13 because that normally that solves the problem in short order. Unlike Chapter 7, there are no provisions in the laws governing Chapter 13 cases that allow a creditor to object to a plan on the grounds of fraud or intentional wrongdoing. The only objection that can be raised is that the Chapter 13 was brought in bad faith. In most cases, however, even if the debtor has fraudulently taken money from a creditor, he is likely filing the Chapter 13 with every intention of making it work. Hence an objection by the wronged creditor won't stop his Chapter 13 case from proceeding. As effective as Chapter 13 is at saving the hide of imprudent contractors, it doesn't stop criminal prosecution.

Several years ago I got a frantic phone call from a contractor who had underbid a string of jobs and was at the end of the line. Unfortunately, this last owner hired an astute attorney who knew that what the contractor had done was not only fraudulent, but violated a criminal statute. He knew the contractor didn't have any money and probably couldn't pay a judgment, so he had his client contact the DA and file criminal charges. My client was flabbergasted because he didn't see himself as a criminal. After all, what he had done was a pretty common practice among his peers. But the owner and his attorney wouldn't back off, and the District Attorney pressed on with the criminal prosecution.

Terrified of the prospect of going to jail, my client begged his family and friends to bail him out and they did. With money in hand we offered it to the owner with the stipulation that he would sign a non-prosecution affidavit. He agreed and my client tendered the money. This didn't guarantee that the DA would dismiss the case, but normally they will if the plaintiff asks them to and there has been restitution.

So, the question is: Why do contractors underbid a job? Many times it is done inadvertently, because either the owner or the estimator doesn't understand how to determine the total costs of doing a job, or is overly optimistic in calculating the time it will take to get it done. But sometimes its not the fault of the bidder.

Joel Johnston is a case in point. Joel called me one day to tell me he'd been sued. A few hours later when he came in I asked him what the lawsuit was all about.

"About year and a half ago I was awarded all the electrical work on a new school being built. If the contractor would have started the job right away, I would have been alright. But he delayed the project eighteen months and during that time the cost of materials went up fifty percent. There is no way I can do the job without losing a ton of money."

"Oh, great. Did you make the bid in writing?"

"Yeah. I wrote it on out on an invoice."

I sighed. "Well, for starters you should have a form specifically for bids and one of its provision should be a time limit, expiration date, or an adjustment provision for increases in material or labor costs. Just writing up a bid on a blank invoice is a pretty sloppy."

"I know but I've been doing that for years and never had a problem."

"So, the contractor is suing for the increased cost in getting the electrical work done?"

"Right."

"Well, how much are we talking about?"

"Forty-two thousand."

"Hmm."

"So, what can I do?" Joel asked meekly.

"Well, since they have sued you, you'll have to defend yourself, but unless you can come up with a good defense you'll just be throwing good money after bad. It would be cheaper just to file bankruptcy assuming your company doesn't have any assets."

"No. I own all my tools and we rent all our equipment."

"Does anyone owe you any money?"

"No. We're between jobs. There a few old debts that we'll probably never collect."

"Then a chapter 7 is the way to go, I think. If you don't have any cash and nobody owes you money, there's nothing to lose. Once someone gets a judgment against a corporation they can make it almost impossible to do business, so you might as well get it over with and move on."

So, as you can see, bidding a job is very complicated and easy to botch. Many small contractors or subcontractors don't keep books or do any kind of cost accounting, so they really don't know how much it costs to complete a job. Oftentimes they fail to take into consideration administrative costs, depreciation of equipment, interest expense, taxes, and other expenses that don't seem directly related to the project.

Another problem with bidding a job is being overly optimistic. Contractors often seem to think it will take less time to finish a job than it actually does. They may underestimate the cost or quantity of materials needed or fail to consider increases in transportation costs. Whereas these entrepreneurs usually do quality work, they very often totally miscalculate the bid and end up in serious trouble.

Recently, I defended a contractor against a sub who had bid too low on a project and ended up spending fifty percent more than he had anticipated. He was an excavator and his mistake was not doing a core sample on this particular project. Shortly after construction began he discovered a layer of rock that required much heavier equipment than he had bid into the job. He immediately went to the contractor and wanted more money, but the contract held his feet to the fire.

Bidding sometimes becomes a game or competition for some entrepreneurs. They forget about the importance of making a profit feeling that they must win at all cost. This is foolish and the entrepreneur may end up bidding the job so low he not only can't make a profit but he can't even finish the job. The short term satisfaction of landing the job will soon fade and when reality sets in, the entrepreneur will be facing a nightmare that may end up putting him out of business, but only after months and months of painful suffering as the business slowly craters.

The solution is to keep a good set of books with accurate cost accounting so that the business owner will know exactly what his or her costs are on each project. Then, when the bid is calculated, profit can be built in to make the whole exercise worthwhile. The owner must resist the temptation to bid the job below cost or with too little profit just to keep busy. If he can't do this, he should turn over the bidding process to someone more objective. Someone who will bid the job strictly on a cost plus profit basis. Whereas the owner is usually the person with the best knowledge of how to do the job, he may be the worst person to bid it.

Underbidding a job is crazy and totally avoidable, at least the second time around. The first time it might be an honest mistake, but after that it's pure stupidity. If the owner bids the job correctly and doesn't get the job, then he has to be able to just shrug it off and go on to the next one. If he bids correctly, but doesn't get any jobs, then he must look at ways to cut his costs or improve his efficiency so he can do the job for less money. But he must be realistic. Just getting a job for the sake of getting it is foolish and an invitation to disaster.

Plastic

They came from everywhere
Over here and over there
The mail, the phone, the mall
Unsolicited, one and all
Get them one, two, or ten
Don't wait—pick up the pen

It's a simply wonderful game
All you do is sign your name
Now jump for joy, and yell hooray!
Cause baby they're on their way
Dillards, Penneys to name a few
Visa, Mastercard, and Amex Blue

You can live the American dream
Stand up now and let out a scream
Buy it now, no money down
You've got credit all over town
Sit back and watch your dreams come true
Don't worry, only pennies due

For Moses it was manna provided by the Lord
No need to sit around the house so bored
Now its silver, gold, and platinum too
Macy's, Sears to name just two
Cars, clothes, a ten day cruise
Gambling, clubs, and lots of booze

You've got it all and then some more
Until the bills flood in the door
It cannot be, I didn't spend that much
Just a few odds and ends and such
Eighteen, twenty, twenty-four
Interest, interest, bills galore

Oh my God, it's all a scam
To steal my life, I'm in a jam
Collectors call day and night
My balances are out of sight
I can't sleep or think
Go to work, eat or drink

My lover scorns me, yells, and screams
God, what happened to my dreams?
Letters come demanding blood,
Tears from my face do flood
My lovers's gone, couldn't take the heat
I'm here alone, tired and beat

Is all that's left bankruptcy?
What was my sin? Idolatry?
I see it now, clear as glass
I fell in love with cold, hard cash
Visa, Mastercard, Amex Blue
Lucifer got his due

6
The Credit Trap

Early on in life all of us are indoctrinated on how important credit is to everyone. We are told over and over again that good credit is the secret to financial success and happiness in life. Every day we are barraged with advertisements for all sorts of expensive luxury items and told we can buy them right now on credit, and nearly everyone takes the bait.

So, we get a house we can't afford, a luxury car we don't need, and run up a half-dozen credit cards to the hilt. Before we know it we're a slave to the banks and financial institutions that have financed our extravagant living. We have stepped into the credit trap meaning from now on a huge chunk of our hard-earned money is going to banks and mortgage companies in interest payments. We pay and pay and pay, yet the balance we owe never goes down. For many of us the joy of life is soon gone—happiness is replaced with constant worry and depression.

Think about it. From the day we are born, we're told that good credit is our ticket to the American dream. We can have all the luxuries and modern conveniences of life on credit. Why wait, they say, when we can have it right now.

Millions of Americans, including myself, have been victimized by this credit conspiracy. The lure of easy money is so tantalizing that few can resist it. As I mentioned, I started my own law practice with a two-thousand dollar cash advance on my American Express card. I tried to get conventional financing but had no collateral, so I was summarily turned down. Over the years, I continued to finance my small business with high-interest credit card debt that the average entrepreneur would have no prayer of ever paying off. In fact, getting the mail was always a risky business. Often when I went out and got it I'd discover I'd received a check made out to me for $10,000-$25,000. All I had to do was deposit it and the money was mine to spend. This will happen to every entrepreneur as soon as they are in business for a while. Of course, I always shredded the checks I got as the attached financial disclosures would indicate the interest rate was 28% or more! But can you imagine if an entrepreneur got a check in the mail like that when he was desperate for money to make payroll or needed to purchase inventory? The temptation to cash that check would be staggering.

Along with the big checks in the mail, there will also be credit card solicitations offering guaranteed acceptance with credit limits of $2,500 to $25,000. Of course, the lowest interest offered again will be 28%. In the first quarter of 2010, according to the marketing intelligence firm, Mintel Compermedia, total credit card direct mail solicitation volume was 1.2 billion pieces! This is an unconscionable abuse by the credit card industry motivated by greed and a reckless disregard for their customers' well-being. At a time when interest rates are ridiculously low, and banks can get all the cheap money they want, they shouldn't be trying to fleece the American consumer. Unfortunately, credit card lending is so lucrative they can't help themselves.

So, I tell my clients they shouldn't feel guilty about filing bankruptcy as they have been lured into this credit trap by greedy lenders who care nothing about their customer's welfare. When creditors lure people into buying things they can't afford and borrowing money they can't realistically pay back, they reap big profits. I guarantee, though, that these finance companies, payday lenders, banks, and credit card issuers will have little sympathy when a customer loses his job or gets sick and can't pay the debt. They will turn on you the moment you get behind on a payment. They'll call and harass you, send you threatening letters, and destroy your credit without giving it a second thought. I see this every day and it sickens me.

So, when the entrepreneur goes out to the mailbox he must marshall all his strength and will power, and do what I do, immediately shred any credit card applications or preauthorized checks that I find. Also, I check my current credit card bills for blank checks the have included, designed to lure me into maxing out my credit cards, and shred them too. You have to be vigilant to avoid this trap.

A few entrepreneurs might be successful at paying off this high-cost debt, but most will eventually perish because of it. Eventually, the burden of the minimum monthly payments will get so heavy that the business will collapse. I remember one bankruptcy client who, to fund his new business, had charged a whopping $150,000 on eleven credit cards all issued by the same company. It amazed me that the credit card company had let him have eleven cards in the first place, but the fact that he was able to run up $150,000 in credit card debt was mind-boggling. During the course of the bankruptcy I fully expected this creditor to come up with some kind of an objection to the bankruptcy but we never heard from them.

Credit cards are very handy for travel, online purchasing and make it easy to keep track of business expenses. But they shouldn't be used for financing your business or covering your negative cash flow at home. If you are using credit cards for this purpose you need to stop immediately and take a close look at the business. Find out what is wrong and correct it, but don't keep digging a hole that will eventually swallow you and your small business.

So, now you've been warned, but will you do anything about it? Probably not. Credit cards are addictive just like cigarettes and booze. They provide immediate pleasure and allow you to fulfill your dreams. In your mind you've got everything under control. You tell yourself that you can stop using your credit cards whenever you want. So, why don't you?

What makes credit cards so dangerous is their simplicity and lack of immediate consequences if they are over used. Unlike booze, there is no immediate hangover to make you regret your actions. The consequences of your indiscretions with your credit card are deferred for months or years. For a while you can manage to make the minimum payments without too much struggle, but eventually all the minimum payments add up and you find yourself overwhelmed.

The use of credit cards defies logic. Why would anyone pay 29% interest, late fees, over the limit penalties, and an annual membership fee, when the bank won't pay you 2% if you buy a CD. It's ludicrous. But when I point it out to clients they just shrug. It's like their minds don't compute when it comes to credit cards. Armed with a pocket full of plastic gods they become mindless zombies who have no idea what they are doing. In a futile effort to get clients to realize the danger of credit card addiction, I wrote a novel called, *Plastic Gods*. It's a financial thriller about an attorney, Rich Coleman, who tries to make it rich by setting up a string of bankruptcy clinics in Texas. In the story his Debt Relief Centers are so effective that local bankruptcies skyrocket threatening the viability of a local subprime lender. Rather than lose this lucrative business the Bank's CEO puts a hit out on Rich hoping this will save his sinking ship.

I can understand turning to credit cards if someone is desperate. It's a quick and easy solution, but I can't understand why many of my bankruptcy clients over the years have turned to pawn loans, payday loans, title loans, or other legalized loan shark operations. Without giving it a second thought they sign a note that provides sometimes over 900% annual interest. What's ridiculous is that the Truth-In-Lending disclosure is right there staring them in the face and they still sign on the dotted line. When a person absolutely has to have money they will usually do whatever it takes to get it, no matter what the consequences.

What is sad is that people often buy goods and services with credit cards that they don't need. They are not desperate people who are buying food, clothing or gasoline to get to work. They are buying gifts they can't afford to give, luxury items they could do without or booze and cigarettes that will eventually kill them. Nor are these people stupid. They are just as often college graduates as high school dropouts. The common thread among them is materialism and a lack of common sense. They like fancy cars, good food, designer clothing, the latest in technology and large, well-furnished homes. If they can't have all these things they are unhappy.

So, what is the answer to the credit card addict? Fortunately, it's an addiction that can be easily ended. All you have to do is quit paying the credit cards. When you do this they soon will lose their magic and you will never buy something you don't need ever again. Even better your credit score will crater so you won't be able to get new credit cards to replace the ones you have lost.

Of course, the downside of this is having to deal with all the angry collection agents who will start hounding you for payments on the now dead cards. They will threaten you will all kinds of horrible things like contacting employers, calling your neighbors, filing liens, garnishments, attachments, and even criminal prosecution. Of course, they can't legally do any of this, but they will do their best to make you believe it will happen if you don't send them money. It may become so bad you will have to file bankruptcy just to get some peace, but bankruptcy is the worst thing for the credit addict.

That's right because as long as your credit is bad you will have no choice but to go straight. But once you file bankruptcy your credit will rebound quicker than you'd ever thought possible and then you'll be right back where you started with a pocket full of plastic gods.

So, rather than going through all of that, the better

move for the credit addict is to simply cut up all the credit cards and pay them off as quickly as possible. This will be painful and require a lot of sacrifice, but it will be well worth it as it will free you from the financial shackles that have bound you from the moment you stepped into the credit trap.

Lucky for me, attorneys often find themselves in a position to make the big score. For me it was a personal injury case that netted enough to pay off my credit card debt and the loan on my home, but it was only after struggling for twenty years that I finally escaped the credit trap and became debt free. For most entrepreneurs bankruptcy or death will be their only way out.

The Banker

If you borrow money
You should be aware
Of the truth about some bankers
Lest you fall into their snare

Interest is their magic wand
That brings them mighty riches
Keep a careful eye on it
Or you'll lose your frickin' britches

Stacks and stacks of papers
They'll thrust into your face
Hoping you won't read them
Cause the loan's a damn disgrace

They'll want your guarantee
Your aunt's and uncle's too
And a pledge of all your assets
I guess, that'll have to do

They'll treat you like a king at first
Smile, pat you on the back
Until something goes awry
Or falls into a crack

Then they'll call you twice a day
To find out what's gone wrong
Gotta have that payment soon
Can't wait, it's been too long

If you ask them for more time
They'll frown and say "no way."
Gotta get the payment now
Can't wait another day

As they haul your assets off
You'll scream and yell in vain
Now that you've got nothin'
You can barely stand the pain

So, now the truth I've told you
Keep a sharp and wary eye
'Cause the thing about your banker
He's slick and very sly

7
Greedy Lenders

In many businesses, financing is absolutely necessary. For instance, doctors and dentists require a lot of expensive equipment to operate their practices. A trucking company or car rental agency obviously will have to finance their vehicles. If your small business requires any kind of financing be careful. Bankers are a greedy bunch, and you will pay dearly for the money you have to borrow. Not only will the interest and fees be outrageous, but they will also want you to pledge every asset you own to secure their loan to you.

The key to negotiating a good loan is to appear not to need the money. Most entrepreneurs wait until they are in desperate need of cash before they go to their banker. Without batting an eye they sign anything their banker sticks in front of them. They rarely read the voluminous paperwork associated with the loan and hardly ever get the advice of an attorney. Few realize how much power they have given to the cold, arrogant banker who cares nothing about them, but only about the big profits his bank will be making off their sweat.

When I read through commercial loan documentation today I am appalled at how the finance industry is taking advantage of the entrepreneur. Not only do banks require far too much collateral, but it is common now for banks to make a borrower waive all defenses and offsets that they might have against the bank, waive the right to a jury trial, waive notice of default, comply with highly complex financial ratios that few of borrowers understand, provide burdensome financial reporting and documentation, and, even in some cases, sign over the business to the bank before they will make the loan.

Borrowing money today is almost as dangerous as smoking cigarettes or snorting cocaine. The entrepreneur may not die from borrowing money, but his business could be snatched away from him in a heartbeat. As soon as he signs the big stack of loan documents his future is in grave danger. In fact, I've found many, if not most, small business loans are in default before the ink is dry. If you read all the onerous provisions and requirements of these documents, few entrepreneurs could ever comply with them. Consequently, the banker has the power to put you out of business at will.

If you make every payment on time you might be okay, but almost every small business owner has cash flow crunches from time and time. Once your payment to the bank gets behind, your business is in serious jeopardy. Whereas some bankers will cut you some slack, just as many won't care about your plight and will pull the choke chain the moment you're a day late or a dime short on a payment.

So, what do you do if you absolutely must have capital for your business? First of all, it's far better to get investors than borrow money. You would be surprised how many of your friends and family would be willing to invest in your business if you would just ask them. Investor money doesn't have to be paid back at any particular time and doesn't accrue interest. This gives the investor-financed business a great competitive advantage in the marketplace.

For instance, the publishing business is a brutally competitive business today. If you walk into any major chain bookstore and look around you will be overwhelmed by the number of titles you have to choose from. The big publishing houses spend hundreds of thousands of dollars to promote many of their front line titles. They have big sales forces and often purchase exclusive use of prime shelf space in the bookstores.

For someone to start a small press in this environment might seem foolhardy, but it is done every day. The entrepreneur in this case has investor money, or is putting up his own money to finance the business. If he had to borrow money, he wouldn't last six months because very little revenue comes in during the first six months of operations in this industry. Even after that, revenue growth is slow, so it's imperative to have a very low overhead.

Those who invest in small businesses are simply betting on the ability of the entrepreneur to make the business a success. Over the years I have helped a number of fortunate entrepreneurs sell their businesses for over a million of dollars. Had these ventures been financed by investment capital rather than commercial loans, the investors would have made a killing. I know of one such investor who has now retired and spends half his time in his million dollar home in Dallas and the other half of his time in his million dollar beach house in Maui.

If you can't find investors, try to get unsecured loans if possible. It's amazing how much money can be borrowed today without putting up collateral. Every week

I get applications in the mail for $25,000-$100,000 unsecured lines of credit. If you have good enough credit to do this and don't have to pay too high an interest rate, then that is the way to go.

If you can't get an unsecured loan, then the next best thing is a loan without recourse. This means your collateral is at risk but the bank can't come after you personally for any deficiency they suffer. In real estate financing I see this type of financing all the time, particularly by life insurance companies. If the bank is anxious to make the loan they might agree to do this if you ask for it. After all, if they have properly appraised the property it should sell for enough to pay of the loan. If the entrepreneur is personally liable on the note it just gives the bank incentive to sell the real estate too cheaply and then collect the difference from the entrepreneur.

If the bank says no, thank them and keep looking for another lender. Patience is very important in acquiring funding for your business. When the bank understands that the non-recourse financing is a deal-breaker, they might change their mind. If not, you're better off to keep looking.

You should always try to avoid personal guarantees. If your business is doing well and has accumulated assets, then it should be able to borrow money on its own financial statement. Don't be intimated by your loan officer. Take charge of the loan application process and tell the bank the loan is between the business and the bank, not with you personally. Why should you have to risk every dime you've earned over the years? Don't give in to your banker's insistence that you personally guarantee every loan. Deal with them business to business and keep your personal balance sheet out of it.

Preparation for obtaining a loan is very important. Before you apply for a loan, you should get with your attorney and set up what I call a defensive estate plan. What this means is that you structure your assets in such a way that they aren't vulnerable to all the predators lurking about who are looking for an opportunity to take them away from you. This is done by setting up a living trust to provide you with a little privacy and a layer of insulation from your predators.

A living trust is simply another legal entity which you control that holds most of your assets. One of its great advantages is the privacy that it provides both while you are alive and if you or your spouse should die. When you give someone a financial statement, all you have to disclose is the value of the living trust ownership interest. There is no requirement that you itemize each asset held in the trust. People may ask you to disclose the trust holdings, but it is your option whether or not to do it. My recommendation is to hold your assets close to your vest. The less the rest of the world knows, the better.

Once everything is in your living trust, it then sets up a family limited partnership. A family limited partnership is simply a limited partnership owned by the entrepreneur and his living trust, or sometimes a corporate general partner and the entrepreneur's living trust. The FLP, as it's called, provides additional privacy, some tax advantages, but most of all, asset protection. This is because many limited partnership statutes do not allow a creditor to seize assets from the FLP, but only to surcharge the partner's interest. This makes it very difficult for a predator to successfully steal assets from an entrepreneur. If you have millions of dollars to protect you might want to consider off-shore trusts for another layer of protection, but this has its risks and drawbacks, so it isn't usually wise for the average entrepreneur.

It is important that any businesses you run are incorporated or are a limited liability company. This will protect any assets in your name as well as those contained in you trust or FLP. Any borrowing should be done by the business entity needing the money. If possible, neither you, your living trust, or the FLP should guaranty any business debt.

Once you have set up your defensive estate plan, you'll want to keep your financial affairs private and only tell lenders as little as possible about the assets you have. Be careful, though, when you fill out a personal or business financial statement for a bank or other lender everything on that financial statement must be accurate and you must fully disclose all of the assets and liabilities of such entity. Providing a false or inaccurate financial statement is a crime and the lender won't hesitate to refer an account to the FBI or state prosecutors if they find out the financial statement provided wasn't correct. I would have your accountant review any financial statements before you give them to the bank.

Remember, your banker will want every asset he knows about as collateral. You have no obligation to tell him what is in your trust or FLP because they are not borrowing the money. If the banker won't lend you what you want without knowing what's in your trust and FLP, go to another bank.

The key to getting a loan on your terms is not to be

desperate. Be prepared to walk away if the bank isn't willing to make the loan documents fair and reasonable. Don't agree to guarantee the loan and only give them a reasonable amount of collateral. If the lender wants to make the loan, they will bend to your will. If they won't be reasonable, find another lender or do without the money.

The Bookkeeper

Sally Ann, that was her name
Pretty and bright, she knew the game
Bookkeeping, typing—she did it all
She lifted our load so we'd stand tall

Happy, relieved we'd found what we sought
We left her alone, scarcely gave her a thought
She was in early each day, left late at night
A hard worker she was, what a delight!

A year went by then cash got so tight
We shuddered to think of our horrible plight
Plenty of business, we all worked hard
Then it hit us, we'd let down our guard

Money is missing, where did it go?
We asked Sally Ann, she said, "I don't know."
Shocked and dismayed at this twist of fate
We poured over the books until very late

Then we saw it, the game she had played
Anger swept o'er us, we had been betrayed
We called our attorney, the sheriff, the DA
She couldn't get away with it, she had to pay

But alas, she was smart and vanished that night
Gone away, far away by dawn's early light
Leaving us reeling, depressed, without hope
Wondering if we'd reached the end of the rope?

8
Theft and Embezzlement

A critical problem for the entrepreneur is finding people they can trust. Nobody can watch every employee every minute. There are a myriad of ways customers and employees can steal from you without being detected. Such was the case for Don and Ho Park, who brought their life's savings from Korea and opened up a janitorial business in Arlington. They felt fortunate when a bright young woman answered their ad for a bookkeeper. She was kind and patient with them and helped them master the English language. She seemed to know all the ins and outs of accounting, payroll and tax compliance, so they left all those matters in her hands. Her salary wasn't cheap but it was reasonable considering all that she did for them.

Business started out slow but grew steadily for several years as they acquired more and more customers. Even though sales were good and overhead was modest, they seemed to always have cash flow problems. Since they didn't understand financial statements or bookkeeping they had no idea what was happening to them. Finally, they started watching the bookkeeper a little more carefully and noticed the deposits she was making were for less than the receipts they were giving her. When confronted with this she confessed that she routinely took ten percent from each deposit and put it into her account. Over the years it had amounted to more than $50,000!

Don and Ho were shocked and horrified by this betrayal. When I suggested they go to the DA, however, they declined because they were so humiliated by what had happened that they didn't want anyone to know about it. I understood how they felt but didn't relish the idea of letting the bookkeeper off the hook so easily. Eventually, Don and Ho were able to pull themselves out of the huge hole that their employee had dug for them, but only because they were running a tight ship and had a lot of friends and family providing a cheap labor pool. A more marginal business wouldn't have been able to survive a $50,000 hit like they did.

There are other, more creative ways to embezzle which are difficult to detect. In a case in Desoto, a convenience store had been in operation for years when the owner, Pete Briggs, decided to move to the country. He turned over the business to a manager who had been with him for several years and he trusted implicitly. Over the next eighteen months or so he discovered his sales were down and wondered what was going on, since business had always been good at this store. When the manager was confronted about the shortage and poor sales he just shrugged and said times were bad.

Later when Peter asked his accountant about the losses, he told him that there was a serious inventory shortage. At this point we were hired to try to get to the bottom of the problem. When we started interviewing employees we discovered that the manager had systematically fired all the old employees and hired members of his own family to work in the store. He also conveniently disabled all the security cameras and claimed they were being repaired.

After inspecting cash register tapes we discovered that there were hundreds of voided transactions, which we suspected meant sales were being made, the tickets voided, and the money pocketed. Unfortunately, when we subpoenaed bank records, we couldn't find any extra cash coming into the account. Since all the employees were related to the manager, they were uncooperative in our investigation. The only explanation we could come up with was that the manager was spending all the money that he was stealing. This certainly was possible, but there was a quarter million dollars missing, so we were pretty sure there must be a stash somewhere.

When we took the deposition of the manager's spouse, we discovered she had her own small landscape business. The business seemed legitimate until we tried to find out who her customers were. She could only name a few and was very vague as to the jobs she had under contract. It soon became clear that the money being embezzled by her husband was being booked as the sales for her landscape business.

In going through her bank statements with her, I noticed several large withdrawals. When I asked her about them, she claimed it was her practice to withdraw large sums to purchase cashiers checks to pay bills. When I pointed out that on several occasions there were no cashier's checks purchased, she admitted to storing the cash in her freezer until she needed it!

During all this time the DA couldn't be bothered with the prosecution of an embezzlement case because he felt it would be too difficult to prove. Eventually the case settled and the client recovered $100,000 of the quarter million embezzlement. Fortunately for my client, his business had a prime location, so he was able to sell his business and recoup his money, but his was a unique case. Most entrepreneurs couldn't survive a quarter million dollar embezzlement, and I know of several who had to file bankruptcy after losing far less than that.

I could go on and on with more tales of employee dishonesty as it is very common. The point I want to make is that embezzlement usually occurs because the entrepreneur is not paying close enough attention to his business. Employees should be carefully screened before they are hired. Resumes should be verified, criminal background checks should be made, and references checked.

Once employees are hired, it's not wise to trust all of the accounting to one person. More than one employee should handle deposits, check-writing, and checkbook reconciliations. Spread the work around to make it difficult for one person to control the system. The owner should always review bank statements for irregularities. Monthly profit and loss statements should be created and routinely reviewed to spot unusual entries or trends. Blank checks should never be written.

I had one client who would routinely sign blank checks whenever she was out of town or on vacation. Her bookkeeper would then pay the bills as they came in. After a few years, when cash flow began to be a problem, the owner started to review her old bank statements. To her shock, she found she had been double paying vendors. When she checked with the vendors they denied being paid twice. Upon checking with the bank, it seems the bookkeeper had set up accounts with names similar to the vendor's and was depositing the extra check into her own accounts.

Usually the bank will have to make good on checks they accept with forged signatures or endorsements, but in this case it was not that simple. The signatures were valid and the bank alleged that our client was negligent in signing blank checks. On the other hand, the endorsements were fraudulent and we alleged that the bank was negligent in letting this employee set up all these bank accounts in fictitious names. The dispute went into litigation which lasted for years. Eventually, the case settled and our client got partial restitution, but the battle cost my client dearly in time, money, and mental distress.

In fact, the woman who had written the blank checks felt so guilty that she became obsessed with the case, calling me every day and sometimes several times a day about it. She wanted the money that she had lost, but more than that, she wanted the bookkeeper to pay. The case was so distracting and mentally debilitating to her that she could scarcely work in the business after this happened.

Your accountant can recommend other measures to protect against employee dishonesty, and these measures should always be implemented. Many people blame their accountant for not detecting embezzlement, but usually the employee is smart enough to hide their handiwork so that the accountant won't readily see it. It's the entrepreneur who has the best shot at detecting dishonesty, because he or she is there every day and should detect any irregularities.

If all else fails, the entrepreneur can get fidelity insurance to cover any losses suffered from employee dishonesty. Generally the insurance is inexpensive and can be attached as a rider to a general liability policy. The sad thing I've found, however, is that very few entrepreneurs have this type of insurance coverage.

9
Competition

Competition is one of the more obvious causes of small business failure. When the big chain store or franchise operation moves in down the street, it's just a matter of time before the small business folds. Cooperative advertising and name recognition give them a competitive advantage. They buy in bigger quantities, which allows them to undercut the prices charged by the small business owner. They have much larger reserves and can keep prices low until they put the entrepreneur out of business. The only defense against this is to run a tight operation and provide better and more personal services to your customers so they will be willing to pay a little more for your product. Customer loyalty takes time to build, but when it is finally achieved, it can provide stability and insulation from competitive forces.

But what I want to concentrate on are those types of competition that you can guard against and do something about should they threaten your small business. These practices are called "unfair competition," and they can literally destroy a small business overnight. They include libel and slander, personnel raiding, breach of confidentiality, dissemination of trade secrets, interference with contract, and price-fixing.

Once, I got a call from a client who was in the

consulting business. The client was very upset because a salesmen in a competitive business was telling the client's existing and potential customers that they had infringed on the competitor's copyright. It was a lie and an obvious attempt to subvert the business relationship of the parties. If this type of slander were allowed to go unanswered, our client would no doubt have lost that customer and maybe the business.

Our response was to send a cease-and-desist letter advising the competitor that our client was prepared to go to court should they persist in slandering our client. In most cases this will stop the unfair business practice but, if it doesn't, it's important to follow through with your threats and seek a temporary injunction. Once the competitor knows you are serious about protecting your rights, they will usually back off.

A more subtle attack on a small business is theft of employees. Almost every business will have one or more key employees who are instrumental to the success of the business. They might be sales representatives, technical personnel, or savvy administrators. The competition soon learns who these people are and will start plotting a way to steal them from you. And if it isn't the competition, often it's one of these employees themselves who suddenly realize they are the key to the businesses' success. So they decide to go out on their own, expecting to get rich themselves rather than make an ungrateful employer rich.

Invariably these key people will try to take others with them. The loss of one or two key employees like this can devastate a business and quickly put it in jeopardy. Luckily, this is a danger that can be easily avoided simply by having properly drafted employment contracts with these key people. These should be drafted carefully by an attorney and include appropriate non-competition, non-solicitation, and non-disclosure agreements. Typically these key employees will be prohibited from going into business in the same territory for several years after their termination, prevented from soliciting employees from the business for this period, and stopped from disclosing any proprietary information or trade secrets learned during their employment.

A lot of times employee disloyalty is due to poor treatment by the entrepreneur. Sometimes, when the employee is first hired, promises are made that haven't been kept or the terms of employment are not clearly laid out in a written contract. One common promise is equity ownership in the business. Employees often think they will be given stock in the company or a percentage of profits. Entrepreneurs may vaguely promise these things verbally to induce the employee to sign on but then conveniently forget about them later.

Every employee the entrepreneur hires should be told the terms of employment up front. These terms should be written down so that both parties can refer to it later if any confusion arises. This can be a one page document that includes salary, overtime policies, explanations of sick time, vacation time, medical insurance, pensions or profit sharing, and temporary disability. The document should state that these are all the terms of employment and that there are no verbal side agreements as to the terms of employment. Finally, the document should state that the employment is at will and the employment can be terminated without cause upon 14-days-notice. This means no reason or explanation for the termination is necessary if the 14-day-notice is given. If the employee has done something wrong, then no notice period is required but an explanation must be given to the employee pointing out the wrongful conduct. If the entrepreneur and the employee sign the document acknowledging these terms of employment there shouldn't be any confusion or misunderstanding about it later.

For key employees particularly those that are with the entrepreneur at its inception, it is important to honor all the promises that have been made to them. Don't be greedy and try to keep all the profits for yourself. If other partners and employees have contributed to the success of the business you should be happy to give them their share of the profits. If you do that they almost always will be loyal to you and everyone will prosper as a result. But if you deny them what they deserve they will be bitter and seek ways to get revenge. If this happens everyone loses.

Theft of proprietary information and trade secrets is another way a small business can be placed in jeopardy. I once represented a software engineer who was employed by a video game company. While employed by the company, the engineer developed video game technology that was state-of-the-art and very valuable. Although the company had paid him everything he was due under his employment contract, he realized how valuable his technology had become and was bitter that he didn't own it. Fortunately for the company, they had a good employment contract which stipulated that any technology developed for the company belonged to the company.

Nevertheless, the employee felt like it was his technology and decided to quit and take the technology to a competitor who would pay him a handsome sum for it. If the employer had allowed this to happen, they not only would have lost the technology, but their competitor would have been in a position to bury them. Because they had properly documented their ownership of the technology, they were able to file a complaint for theft of a trade secret with the local district attorney. This is when I was hired by the employee, who was about to go to jail.

I explained to him that when he accepted employment with his employer, he had sold any rights to anything he developed while being employed by the company. He was bitter because he claimed the owners had promised him stock options, bonuses, and other fringe benefits that they hadn't delivered. This may well have been true, but none of those things were in the employment contract he had signed. I told him his mistake was signing an employment contract without advice of counsel.

A few days later, I arranged an informal negotiation session to try to resolve the dispute. It was a very tense and bitter meeting as both parties had a lot at stake. Finally, we reached a compromise whereby the engineer would get a nice, 90-day severance package to give him time to find a new job, the employer would sign a non-prosecution agreement, and the engineer would acknowledge the company's ownership of the technology. As we were driving away, the engineer let out a sigh of relief. I turned and smiled at him. He said he was glad they had settled, because if they hadn't he was prepared to put them out of business. When I asked him how he could have done that, he said that before he left the company he had sabotaged all the company's computers. He pulled a remote control device from his pocket and waived it in front of me. Then he smiled and said, "Push this little button and all the technology he'd developed would be erased."

10
Misfortune

No small business owner is immune from misfortune. Eventually, it will strike everyone. It always does. Fortunately, misfortune can usually be anticipated, and plans can be made to mitigate its impact. Yet many entrepreneurs totally ignore the risks and dangers inherent in running a business and fail to take any measures to protect themselves.

The worst blow to any small business is the loss of the owner or a key employee. Yet very few small businesses have adequate life and disability insurance on these key figures. If there is insurance, it is purchased to protect the spouse, the children, or a creditor with little thought to what would be necessary to preserve the business itself.

Another common omission is contents insurance. Whereas the landlord usually insures his building, the tenant often doesn't bother to take out a contents policy. If a fire occurs and his business assets are destroyed, he may have no recourse and find himself out of business. Even if the tenant does have contents insurance, rarely is there business interruption insurance. After a fire, a business may be shut down for months and, without income for that period, most businesses will fail or be forced into bankruptcy.

I can remember two of my clients who suffered this

fate. One was an immigrant from China who had established a very nice computer training school in North Dallas. His training was first-class and in high demand. Unfortunately, one night there was a fire in his office building. When he went to work he found his business totally destroyed. He had bought fire insurance to replace his computers and equipment and even had business interruption insurance, but hadn't understood the extent of coverage. When he finally got the proceeds from his insurance it wasn't enough to pay even half the debts he had racked up while he was shut down.

Unfortunately, insurance agents, like other professionals, vary in their knowledge and expertise. Sadly, I have run across many incompetent insurance agents. Be sure your insurance agent is experienced and knowledgeable and make sure you understand exactly what will be covered by your policies. I know it's tempting just to let the agent handle it, but you need to ask a lot of questions and go through various scenarios so you understand exactly what reimbursements you will be getting. Also, be sure and follow-up on the issuance of the policies. There are scam artist out there who sell policies but never place them with an insurance carrier. They collect the premiums but when you have a loss the insurance company declines coverage because the agent failed to remit the premiums and get the policy bound.

I remember getting a frantic call from a software engineer I had represented when he terminated his employment with his company and went to work for a competitor. He had bought a new car for his son who was going off to college in the Midwest. Of course, he had to have insurance for the vehicle so he bought a policy from an agent who had been recommended to him. A week or two earlier his son had been in an accident and the driver of the automobile he'd hit had died. He'd given everyone his insurance information but was shocked to find out the insurance company had no policy in his name. When I confronted the agent he promised to get the matter straightened out but never did. Later on, when I talked to the State Board of Insurance I found out this wasn't the first time this agent had been in trouble and that his insurance license had been revoked.

There is never a happy ending to a story like this. We sued the agent and got a big judgement but it turned out to be worthless because the agent had no assets. Ordinarily, my client's son could have filed bankruptcy but since the police found empty beer cans in the car and had been charged with DUI, it was likely the judgment against him would not have been dischargeable. Eventually the estate settled for an assignment of the judgment against the agent since there were no other assets to go after.

So, be sure after you buy your insurance that you actually get a policy in the mail from the insurance carrier and, if you haven't ever heard of the company, check it out and be sure it is a reputable company. That can be done easily today just by going on the internet to A.M. Best Company or checking with your state's insurance regulator.

Another sad story was that of Jason Baker. He had worked all his life in the grocery business. He'd started out stocking the store part time when he was a teenager, was promoted to checker after graduating from high school, and married another checker named Alice.

They were married, raised a family together and worked side by side at the Corner Market for nearly twenty years. Although they enjoyed their job, their dream was to someday open up their own store.

This opportunity finally materialized when the store's current owner unexpectedly died. Although his widow had other offers for the business, she knew Jason and Alice very well and agreed to sell it to them rather than to a stranger. With their life savings and money borrowed from family and friends they raised the down payment, signed a note to the widow for the balance and closed on the store. They were ecstatic over their new business and had great expectations of success.

For several years the Corner Market did very well and Jason and Alice were very happy. Then one cold winter night there was an electrical short that caught the store on fire. Jason got the call from a police dispatcher early the next morning.

"Mr. Baker?"

"Yes."

"Are you the owner of the Corner Market downtown?" she asked.

"Yes, I'm am. What's wrong?'

"I'm sorry to be the bearer of bad news, but your fire alarm sounded about twenty minutes ago and two trucks were dispatched to your store."

"Oh, my God! How bad is it?"

"I'm not sure, sir, but they've called in for help from another station. You should get over there."

Needless to say Jason and Alice were horrified when they arrived on the scene and found their beautiful store gutted. Although they had adequate fire insurance, they hadn't purchased business interruption insurance. When I asked them about it later, they said they didn't even know that type of coverage existed. Although they immediately contacted their insurance carrier and got right on the reconstruction of the market, it took months and months to complete. In the meantime their customers had no choice but to find other places to buy groceries and when the store finally reopened sales were barely half what they'd been before the fire.

With sales so far down it wasn't six months before they had exhausted all their cash and were forced into a Chapter 11 to keep the business opened. Unfortunately, in order for a Chapter 11 to be successful a business has to become profitable soon after the commencement of the case. Jason and Alice worked hard to restore their sales but they couldn't get it back to the level it was prior to the fire. Consequently, after six month they hadn't been able to come up with a viable plan to propose to creditors and ultimately had to convert to Chapter 7 and close the business.

Another danger to entrepreneurs is employees. Employees have a propensity for being injured on the job and expect the employer to take care of them until they recover, even if it was their own fault they were injured. The workman's compensation system was developed to protect the employer from this potentially devastating liability, but over the years the cost of workman's compensation insurance has become cost prohibitive in the eyes of many entrepreneurs. Because of this, many entrepreneurs have elected to opt out of the system and go naked or provide an alternate plan to deal with on-the-job injuries.

Most of these alternative plans do not provide anywhere near the protection that a regular workman's compensation policy would provide. Consequently, many entrepreneurs facing substantial employee claims can be literally put out of business because the law provides that without workman's compensation coverage, all common law defenses the employer would normally have are lost.

Another pitfall that entrepreneurs often stumble into is terminating employees while on workman's compensation or with an outstanding claim for an on-the-job injury. It's often difficult for an employer to continue to pay an employee who has been injured and can't perform his or her job. I frequently receive calls from my clients asking if they can terminate an injured employee, particularly if it is clear he would never be able to resume his job. I have to tell them they can't do this because injured employees may be protected by the American Disabilities Act or state statutes, and employers can be sued if they wrongfully terminate an employee who is physically impaired. This is extremely frustrating to my clients and difficult for them to accept.

It is particularly bad when the employer thinks the employee has faked the injury. One client, a rather outspoken owner of a chain of dry cleaners in Dallas called me one Monday morning and said an employee had reported an injury while bending down to pick up a basket of clothing. The employee reported that as he straightened up he felt something pull in his back and felt a sharp pain. Of course, there were no witnesses to this injury. The client was convinced the injury took place over the weekend while the employee was gardening at home because a coworker had heard the employee talking to someone about it.

When my client heard of this, he got very angry and fired the employee. Unfortunately, the coworker who heard the admission was an illegal immigrant and was afraid to testify. This was before the ADA but Texas had a statute prohibiting terminating someone who had a valid workmen's compensation claim. So, it wasn't long before my client was served with a lawsuit for wrongful termination. The lawyer who handled the case for the employee specialized in this area and took all his cases on a contingent-fee basis. The law was so much in favor of the employee that this attorney found it a very lucrative business to prey on entrepreneurs struggling to keep their labor costs down.

So, it's important for the entrepreneur not to let his emotions cloud his business judgment. Buy the insurance you need and let the insurance adjusters handle the claims. Although workmen's compensation insurance isn't cheap, in the long run it's better to have the coverage to avoid a catastrophic claim that could jeopardize the business. Entrepreneurs are an optimistic bunch and often delude themselves into thinking disaster won't strike them. But they are wrong; it's just a matter of time until it strikes everyone.

Another pitfall for any small business is undocumented workers. It's tempting to hire illegal aliens without green cards because the perception is that cheap labor will give you a leg up on the competition and improve the bottom line. This may be true initially but eventually the entrepreneur will get caught and face severe, if not catastrophic, consequences for his imprudence. What can go wrong if you hire undocumented workers?

First of all there are severe fines imposed for blatantly violating the law. Up to a $1,000 per employee for a first offense, up to $5,000 per employee the second time it happens, and $10,000 per employee if an employer is still in business for the third infraction. An entrepreneur can even end up in jail if the fines don't deter him. Secondly, the employer will face wage and hour violations. The employees will file claims for the difference between what was paid to them and the minimum wage plus any overtime due. Thirdly, the IRS will likely come down on the entrepreneur for failing to withhold social security, medicare, and federal taxes. Since the entrepreneur is required by law to withhold, the IRS will simply assess whatever should have been withheld to the employer even though the employer has already paid the full amount to the worker. Finally, by not properly processing these undocumented workers through the payroll system they won't be eligible for workmen's compensation, healthcare coverage, or unemployment. The ramifications of any one of these could be staggering in and of itself. So, it is obviously foolish to employ undocumented workers, yet entrepreneurs do it all the time at great peril to themselves and the employees who they employ.

PART 2 - FIGHTING FOR SURVIVAL

Chill, It's No Big Deal

Get a nasty letter in the mail?
Send us money or we'll give you hell?
Don't lose your cool, don't get upset
Chill, it's no big deal

Creditor called and wants his bread?
Got to have it now, no more said?
Don't get upset, don't be depressed
Chill, it's no big deal

Constable come knocking at your door?
You've been sued, can't take no more?
Take a deep breath, don't despair
Chill, it's no big deal

Didn't pay your taxes? Owe a lot?
Accounts been seized. Checks are hot?
Take a walk, get some air
Chill, it's no big deal

Rent is late? Landlord lookin' for the cash?
Wants the rent or you're out on your ass
Take two aspirin and go to bed
Chill, it's no big deal

'Cause when your world starts to crumble
Your lawyer will be sure you don't stumble
He'll smile as he takes your cash and tell you
Chill, it's no big deal

11
It's Not as Bad as it Looks

Before I discuss the fundamentals of operating a small business successfully, I want to discuss what to do when the lights go out, the landlord locks you out, the IRS attaches your bank account or some other catastrophic event occurs. Do you fold up your tent and start looking for a new job? Or are there ways to salvage this most precious asset you have worked so hard to build?

Fortunately, most situations look a lot worse than they are. I often receive frantic calls from clients who think their world has come to an end. Faced with IRS garnishment, lawsuits, foreclosures, repossessions, or attachments, they feel like their world is collapsing around them and that all hope has been lost. One such case was an owner of a cab company, Helen Holmes, who called me, frantic, one afternoon after the constable had just carted off everything in her offices.

Helen and her husband had immigrated to America from the Iraq ten years earlier. They had invested their life's savings along with several hundred thousand dollars from other members of their family in a taxi cab business in North Dallas. It was their hope and dream, that once the business was established and making money, to bring the entire family to the United States. Six months into the venture Helen realized her husband didn't have what it took to be a successful entrepreneur. He was more interested in going out with his buddies and picking up pretty American girls than running a business.

Soon, Helen filed for divorce and was awarded the business. She did pretty well considering she'd had no training in running a business but made a fundamental mistake in ignoring a lawsuit that had been filed against her. It's amazing how many entrepreneurs think that if they don't pick up their certified mail or ignore a citation served upon them, that nothing will happen to them. This head-in-the-sand mentality is a sure ticket to disaster as Helen found out when the constable showed up with two big trucks to haul away all the company's personal property.

Running a cab company with no radio equipment or telephones is rather difficult, so it was critical to get everything returned immediately. I only knew of two ways to accomplish that: pay off the judgment that is being executed or file a Chapter 11. Since Helen was essentially broke, Chapter 11 was the only thing that we could do. Several days later the company's property was returned and she was back in business.

The key to surviving any catastrophe is to keep calm and get professional help immediately. If it's a medical emergency, you call an ambulance or go to the emergency room. When you get served with a lawsuit you should immediately call an attorney so that the suit can be defended. Don't think you can be your own attorney. The law is very complicated and the procedure for prosecuting and defending lawsuits is very precise. An individual without legal training isn't going to be able to put up an effective defense. Another one of my clients,

Art Snider, found this out the hard way.

One evening I was just pulling into my garage when my cell phone rang. I answered the call and it was a man frantic because his business had just been put into a receivership. His name was Art and he'd been referred by an old client. A receivership is where a third party, appointed by the court, is placed into control of a business for the benefit of creditors. Usually the creditor has to get a judgment before it can ask for a receivership.

Art was a young man who ran a financial consulting business. I thought this ironic that a financial consultant had let his business get put into receivership, but I kept my thoughts to myself not wanting to hurt his feelings. Art was outgoing, sincere and quite open. He was very proud of his business and completely humiliated by the receivership.

When I asked him how it had happened he confessed that he had been sued and tried to defend the suit himself to save money. Unfortunately, the opposing counsel was a ruthless attorney who walked right over him in court and soon had control of his business. Receiverships are rather rare today and, had my client retained an attorney, he probably would have been able to successfully avoid the appointment of the receiver. Again, in this situation a Chapter 11 was the only way to stop the receivership and get this client back in control of his business.

When calamity strikes, the key to successfully dealing with it is to get an attorney immediately, identify your adversaries, weigh all the options available, and then pick an appropriate course of action.

Determining your adversaries is pretty easy as

they are usually banging on the door. But sometimes adversaries aren't aggressive and may not have made any noise yet. It's important to do a complete analysis of all your creditors and contractual obligations to see what other potential claims there might be coming your way.

In Helen Holmes' case it wasn't her creditors who turned out to be her worst enemy, but Sunny Cab Company, a competitor owned by an Iranian immigrant, Sam Soli. Sam tried hard to torpedo her Chapter 11 reorganization because Helen's cab company was his most troublesome competitor. Early on Helen's husband had borrowed money from Sam, so he used his position as an unsecured creditor to oppose everything we did in the bankruptcy case and drum up opposition to our plan. Fortunately, after a very hotly contested confirmation hearing, the case was confirmed as the judge saw through Sam's opposition to the plan as being motivated by his own self-interest rather than the interest of unsecured creditors in general.

Another common crisis for the entrepreneur is the IRS garnishment of the company's bank account. Although this is annoying and will cost you whatever cash was in the bank account on the day it was served on the bank, the garnishment is not usually a devastating blow. The short term solution is to set up another bank account. That will work until IRS discovers your new account. But if a business owner can't pay his payroll taxes it's a good sign he's got other problems as well. The landlord may be about to lock him out or his vehicles may be in jeopardy of being repossessed.

Landlords don't usually lock tenants out until they are very far behind on their rent. Trying to collect back rent from an evicted tenant is usually a waste of time, so the landlord usually cuts the tenant a lot of slack hoping he'll get back on track. In a casual conversation with an accountant who had his office across the hall from me, he confessed he was thirteen months behind on his rent. I was shocked at this revelation as I had been a few days late in the past and the landlord had come down on me pretty hard. Like many landlord's he was all bark and no bite, as they say.

Of course, collection habits of landlord's vary a lot so you can't count on them being lenient. A lot depends on the economy and how quickly the landlord thinks he could re-lease the space. If the market is slow he might be more lenient hoping you will turn your business around and get caught up. On the other hand, if office space is scarce he might be anxious to evict you so he can get a paying tenant in the space.

Vehicle repossessions also present a major problem for the entrepreneur. The car that takes you back and forth to work, the truck that delivers your goods to your customers or the forklift that restocks your warehouse are all essential to your operations. If the entrepreneur gets too far behind on his payments the lender may come looking for the vehicle to repossess and sale at auction. Once you know the lender is looking for a vehicle or piece of equipment to repossess simply keeping it out of sight can delay the loss of that equipment for weeks or month. In my experience rarely does a secured creditor go to court seeking a writ of sequestration requiring the surrender of collateral. This could be due to the fact that it is expensive to hire an attorney to try to gain possession of collateral and not always worth the effort. This will particularly be true if the loan is several years old and the collateral has depreciated in value.

Once you become aware of your crisis you should face it and decide on a course of action, and don't delay it's implementation. Time is always of the essence when it comes to defending yourself from attack. For instance, if you owe income taxes, the timing of filing your bankruptcy might be critical. Normally taxes are a priority debt but if they are more than three years old, they become an unsecured debt. It's always desirable to have taxes classified as unsecured because that means they don't have to be paid in full. Taxes, however, become secured if the government files a federal tax lien. Fortunately, the IRS usually isn't too quick to file these federal tax liens, but once they do file them, the taxpayer will likely have to pay the full taxes, plus penalty and interest. This happened in a recent case when a client came to see us about a Chapter 7 bankruptcy. His only creditor was the IRS, and most of the taxes were over three years old. Unfortunately, he had waited several months to deal with the problem. After we had all the papers together and were about to file the bankruptcy, he got a notice that a federal tax lien had been filed. With a lien filed, the bankruptcy wouldn't do him any good because the taxes were now secured by the equity in his homestead.

Another instance in which time is critical is with vehicles that are in danger of repossession. Often people wait until the repo man is stalking them before they contact us. A Chapter 13 usually solves this type of creditor problem, but it's important to file it before the vehicle is taken. Once the car is gone, there is danger that it can be sold and lost forever.

Normally a bank or finance company only has to give a borrower ten days' notice of a private sale. If the sale takes place before the Chapter 13 is filed, the car may be lost. If the car is still in the possession of the bank or finance company when the bankruptcy is filed, then the car can't be sold without court permission. This usually affords the borrower the opportunity to get the car back but, if the creditor resists, an adversary proceeding seeking a turnover of the property, may have to be instituted. Of course, this involves time and money and may not be successful.

So the bottom line is that a small business owner should always react quickly to the first sign of trouble, identify its source, and deal with it quickly and effectively with whatever professional help that is needed.

12
Uncle Sam, the Sleeping Giant

Another common killer of small businesses is taxes. Instead of accepting the fact that taxes must be paid or structuring their business to avoid taxation, small business owners invariably will try to figure out a way not to pay them or feign ignorance as to their obligation to pay them. There are many different types of taxes most of which are complicated and their compliance extremely tedious.

What makes matters worse is that most government tax collectors are understaffed and often slow to do their job. They frequently let entrepreneurs get hopelessly behind before they come down on them. Many times clients have come to me when they owe fifty or a hundred thousand dollars in back payroll taxes. With penalties and interest accruing, there is no way they will ever be able to pay the taxes they owe. Often they have no understanding of how to handle payroll, calculate withholding, or making tax deposits. Consequently they have no idea they are getting themselves in deep trouble.

Paul Ramirez is a prime example. Paul came to me when he was audited by IRS. He was a landscape contractor and had a crew of contract laborers.

"According to your audit notice," I said, "the IRS is disputing that your employees are contract laborers."

"What do you mean? Of course they are," Paul

argued.

"Do you even know what a contract laborer is?"

"Sure. It means they pay their own taxes."

I laughed. "Well, the IRS assumes everyone working for you is an employee. The burden is on you to prove they are not."

Unfortunately, a lot of entrepreneurs don't bother to find out what it takes to qualify a worker as contract labor and Paul was no exception. They just hear from their friends and fellow entrepreneurs that it is a lot cheaper and much less complicated to deal with independent contractors rather than employees.

"How do I do that?" Paul asked.

"There are a dozen or so criteria taken into consideration in determining if a worker is an independent contractor. Most importantly the contractor must (1) actually work for more than one employer, (2) be on his or her own schedule, (3) not be supervised by the employer, (4) not be subject to being fired, and (5) he must use his own tools and equipment. There are others, but these are the most important ones."

Paul just stared at me for a moment. "Well, I just tell them where to go and they do the job. I don't supervise them."

"Right, but do they work exclusively for you?"

"Yes," Paul admitted.

"And you hire and fire them, right?"

He nodded. "They usually just quit. I hardly ever fire anybody."

"What about supplies and equipment?"

"I provide them."

"Well, I'm afraid your men are employees. I can't

really see you winning that battle with IRS."

"So, what do I have to do to make them independent contractors for future years? Paul asked.

"Well, for starters you should have a written contract with each of them that clearly states they are independent contractors. I suppose you would have to pay them by the job rather than hourly and let them do the work on their own timetable."

"I could do that," Paul noted.

"It should provide that they are free to do jobs for other parties and that they must furnish their own equipment."

"They pretty much work on their own anyway."

"But even if you do all that there is no guarantee that IRS still won't challenge it, particularly if you are the only one they do work for. You would really have to strictly follow the terms of the contract and pray it worked. If it didn't and IRS challenged what your were doing they could assess all the taxes you didn't withhold along with penalties and interest against you. It could be a disaster."

"If they were really independent contractors, couldn't you appeal their decision?"

"Sure, you can fight it out in tax court but that would be very expensive and you still might lose. Your best bet is to treat them as employees, do the proper withholding and put them on your workman's compensation policy. In the long run, it's the cheapest and safest way to go."

"Okay, So what do we about the audit?" Paul asked..

"Well, we can try to convince the revenue agent that your employees are independent contractors, but if we fail you better be ready to pay the assessment."

Paul groaned but nodded. Miraculously, the revenue agent who did the audit was within two weeks of retirement and didn't feel like tackling the independent contractor issue with us. After spending two weeks in my office conference room he finally came out and announced he was concluding the audit with a no-change recommendation. We quickly agreed and that was the end of it. Paul had dodged a bullet but I warned him not to press his luck.

Property tax collectors in Texas are even slower than the IRS in going after the taxes that are owed. I've had clients come in who haven't paid property taxes in four or five years and nothing has happened to them. When the taxing authority finally gets around to turning the matter over to an attorney, the amount due is so high the taxpayer can't come up with the money owed.

In Texas, the State Comptroller over the years has been the most aggressive tax collector off all the governmental agencies. Frequently, I get calls from clients who have or are about to have their businesses shut down because they haven't filed their sales tax returns or paid the taxes due. Luckily, the Comptroller hasn't let them get too far behind, so in most cases they quickly pay up. Once they realize they have to file the returns timely and pay the tax, they adjust to it and it has little impact on their business.

Because an entrepreneur can operate for years without paying property taxes or properly reporting and paying payroll taxes, the government ends up financing their businesses. Most of the time entrepreneurs don't realize the business is losing money because they are not paying all their expenses. If they are on a cash basis for accounting purposes, which is common for small businesses, they may well feel like they are profitable when they are not.

Almost every Chapter 11 or 13 that I file for my small business clients involves substantial payroll tax liability issues. Tax liability has often been the primary reason a bankruptcy was necessary. For the entrepreneur, collecting taxes for the federal government is a difficult, complicated, and hazardous task. It's a shame that a better system can't be found for handling this task. In the past, the government's response has been to increase the penalties and interest for not properly reporting and paying payroll taxes. This just makes matters worse, because when the entrepreneur finally resigns himself to paying the tax, the amount due is often double or triple the original tax liability and growing at a stunning rate. Even if the entrepreneur wanted to pay, he has no possible way of doing it short of bankruptcy.

In recent years Congress has changed the tax laws to require more frequent payroll deposits. This is a better approach, but one still difficult to enforce. Perhaps what needs to be done is to require a small business license which requires them to pass a test to show that they have a full understanding of how the tax system works and their responsibilities to pay and collect taxes for the government.

We require people to understand the driving laws before we let them out in the street, so why not make sure they understand the tax laws and other laws pertinent to operation of a small business?

A small business test would be a win-win solution because most entrepreneurs want to be successful and want to pay all their bills. Rarely do I come across a business owner who is intentionally trying to evade taxes. Usually clients get into tax traps out of ignorance or because, when times get tough, they know the IRS will be the last one to come down on them. Optimistic by nature, the entrepreneur believes in his heart that before the hammer will fall, his business will turn around and he'll be able to pay his taxes.

Of course, the other solution is to take this liability off the shoulders of entrepreneurs and eliminate the income tax altogether. But until that happens every entrepreneur needs to learn how the tax systems works, accept the fact that these taxes must be paid, and then make it his first priority to properly report and pay them. If this is too difficult, then the easy solution, and the one I use, is to hire a payroll service to deal with it. These services are generally very cheap when you consider the burden they take off the entrepreneur's shoulders, and they will allow him to focus on more important aspects of his small business like sales and marketing or research and development.

13
Dealing with an Angry Revenue Officer

Any entrepreneur who has dealt with a revenue officer from the IRS collection branch knows it isn't a pleasant experience. More importantly, it's very dangerous because, from the moment the conversation begins, the agent's primary purpose is to get information from the taxpayer that will help in collecting the taxes. That's why a small business owner should never meet with the IRS alone. The first thing they should do when they get a notice, phone call, or visit from a revenue officer, is to call their accountant or attorney.

It's very easy for an unsuspecting taxpayer to give an agent incorrect or misleading information simply because of the pressure, anxiety, and anger the taxpayer may be feeling. The taxpayer is frequently so intimidated that the only thought on his mind is to give the agent whatever he wants and get rid of him. This can be disastrous, as agents often get evidence against you from material they never requested in the first place. Worse yet, they may find evidence pointing to problems in previous years or matters that weren't even the subject of their inquiry.

If possible, the taxpayer should avoid the meeting entirely and let the tax professional handle it. After all, the owner's time is best spent in sales, marketing, and production, and they should avoid distractions when professionals can be hired to deal with them. An owner has enough pressure and stress just operating the business without having unpleasant confrontations with revenue officers.

Once your tax professional determines what tax liabilities you have, there are numerous ways to deal with it. The most frequent is a simple installment agreements. These can either be negotiated or unilateral agreements. A negotiated installment agreement is one that your tax professional works out with IRS for the payment of taxes over a period of time, usually less than a year. For an agreed periodic payment, the IRS agrees to leave you alone. If you miss a payment or fail to fully comply with the tax laws in the future, the installment agreement will be terminated.

Many of my clients have suffered because of this rule. I can think of two clients who owed the IRS over a hundred thousand dollars and had somehow managed to get a revenue officer to agree to a $500 per month installment payout. This payment, of course, didn't even pay the interest on the amount due, but because the client convinced them that it was the best they could do, the revenue officer agreed to it.

Incredible as it may seem, both of these clients allowed their agreements to be terminated because they failed to timely file a subsequent tax return! Once the agreement was terminated, the IRS assigned new revenue agents who weren't nearly as generous as the former ones.

The first thing that is required in a negotiated installment agreement is the completion of a detailed financial questionnaire, Forms 433A or B. You must disclose to the IRS your complete financial situation or they won't even talk to you. Once this has been done there are formulas that determine what amount of money you must pay each month. This amount will invariably be much higher than you had expected and often is a very unrealistic number.

If you can't reach an agreement or you don't want to disclose all your finances to IRS, I often recommend a unilateral agreement. The way this works is you determine how much you can pay each month and just start making those payments. If the period is six months or a year, often IRS won't take any enforcement action against you and you've avoided close IRS scrutiny. A lot of times negotiating an installment agreement will take that long anyway. This doesn't always work, but many times it will, simply because the IRS can see by your regular monthly payment that you are trying. Because they are so understaffed and overworked, it just stands to reason that the taxpayer who is making an effort to pay his or her taxes won't be as high a priority as the one who is not.

If an installment payout is not feasible because of the amount of tax due or you're assigned an unsympathetic revenue officer, the next possibility is an Offer in Compromise. This is a formal proposal to the IRS to pay them less than what is due. One advantage of an Offer in Compromise is that once it is properly submitted all enforcement action stops. That means if your wages are about to be garnished, your bank account attached, or real property is about to be seized, such action will be halted while the Offer in Compromise is being considered.

This is particularly advantageous as it often takes the IRS six months to a year to consider the offer. If the offer is rejected, you can appeal it and get another six months reprieve from paying the tax. And the chances are better at the appellate level that the offer will be accepted as the revenue officers assigned there are more sophisticated, objective and less emotional.

Unfortunately, there are serious disadvantages to an Offer in Compromise: the interest continues to accrue, you must agree to extend the statute of limitations while the offer is being considered, and any failure to file future returns or pay subsequent taxes can cause the revocation of the agreement. So, unless you are very confident an Offer in Compromise will provide you the time you need to pay the taxes or that it will be accepted, it's not a wise move.

So, how do you know whether IRS will accept an offer or not? That's not an easy question. Much depends on whose hands the offer ends up in. Some revenue officers are very rational and reasonable. Others are unsympathetic and arbitrary. I have found that an offer will likely be accepted if: (1) it's unlikely the taxpayer will be able to pay the tax, (2) there is a question of whether the tax is really legitimate, or (3) the taxpayer offers to pay the tax over a period of time and obviously doesn't have the ability to pay it in a lump sum.

In the first instance, if the taxpayer is aged, permanently disabled, or incompetent the IRS will probably accept any reasonable Offer in Compromise because they know that it will be more than they would be likely to collect anyway.

Secondly, if the revenue officer considering the

offer suspects the taxes weren't legitimate in the first place, he or she might agree to an offer that provides for the payment of the correct amount. A common example is when the taxpayer is assessed additional taxes based on erroneous information the IRS received from a third party, but fails to dispute it. If the revenue officer is provided proof that the information given them was wrong, he or she may agree to the offer even though it is too late to dispute the assessment.

This is one positive thing I've learned about the IRS. If you can convince them that the taxes shouldn't have been assessed in the first place, they will often abate the tax even though legally it's too late to contest it. I don't think they have to do this, but I have found they often will.

Finally, if the taxpayer acknowledges they owe the tax but just needs some time to pay it, usually an Offer in Compromise that provides for an installment payout of up to three years can be worked out. Whether interest continues to accrue during this time is negotiable. Sometimes even penalties can be knocked off as part of the agreement.

Although some tax practitioners advertise that they often are able to routinely negotiate payouts of 25 to 33 cents on the dollar, I haven't been able to do that. Usually, if a client is younger than 60, in good health, and employable, the IRS is not likely to accept an Offer in Compromise for less than what is owed. Perhaps the people advertising the ability to get large percentage reductions have connections in the IRS. I have found that former revenue officers or high officials in the IRS who retire into private practice often do have connections that give them an advantage over the rest of us. If you find someone like that, hire them and take advantage of their special relationship. I would keep copies of their advertisements, newsletters and brochures and ask for references though, to be sure they can really deliver the deal they say they can. If it turns out they can't deliver on their promises you'll have the ammunition you'll need to demand your money back.

A final word about the IRS. Don't be intimidated by them. They are just another creditor. They have to abide by rules and regulations just like the rest of us. The key is to get professional help immediately and respond timely to whatever they throw at you. With the IRS, time is usually in your favor, so develop a long-term strategy to deal with your tax problem and stick with it.

Bankruptcy is often your best bet when it comes to dealing with a serious tax issue. Many taxes, such as income taxes, are dischargable if more than three years has elapsed since they were assessed. Even if the taxes are not dischargable, a Chapter 11 or 13 offers the ability to pay out whatever is owed over a period of three to six years. Chapter 13 even provides for the payment of the tax liability without interest! This is because penalty and interest is usually an unsecured debt and unsecured creditors often get a dividend of less than ten cents on the dollar.

Whether a small business owner must file a Chapter 13 or 11 depends on several factors. If the business is a corporation, limited liability company, or partnership, a Chapter 11 would most likely be required. If the owner is operating as a sole proprietor, then a chapter 13 would be appropriate unless his unsecured debt is over $394,725 or secured debt is over $1,184,200 (good through 2019, such sums adjusted every 3 years for inflation.) In this case the entrepreneur would have to file Chapter 11.

What makes a bankruptcy attractive, beyond the ability to pay out the amount due, is the automatic stay. This is a court injunction which prohibits creditors, including the IRS and other taxing authorities, from taking any enforcement action against the person filing the bankruptcy, who is called "the debtor." This relief is extremely important in that it allows the entrepreneur-debtor to get all his creditors off his back so he can concentrate on repairing his troubled business.

The downside with bankruptcy, of course, is the damage it does to a business owner's credit. Many times, however, the credit has already been damaged if a tax lien has been filed, a car repossessed, or an account garnished. Whereas a bankruptcy may be on an entrepreneur's record for up to ten years, a lot of creditors will still give an entrepreneur credit after the bankruptcy is over. As time goes on, more and more creditors will consider an entrepreneur for credit if he has a good job and hasn't run up a lot of new debt. In fact, many bankruptcy clients are astounded when just several months after they file bankruptcy they start getting pre-approved credit card applications in the mail!

Bankruptcy doesn't carry the tremendous stigma that it did in years past. Over a million and a half people file bankruptcy each year, so many banks and financial institutions are tapping into this market. They are willing to take the risk of loaning to this segment of the population because the potential profits are so great.

There will be restrictions, of course, bigger down payments required, and higher interest rates, but at least there will be lenders out there willing to provide financing if it is really needed.

14
State and Local Taxes

Whereas state and local taxes aren't likely to put a small business under, they can cause the entrepreneur a lot of grief if they are overlooked or ignored. Fortunately, in Texas there is no state income tax. For entrepreneurs in other states, reporting and paying state income taxes can be nearly as burdensome as federal payroll taxes. The key, again, is to accept the fact that these taxes have to be paid, and withhold and make deposits each pay period so there is little opportunity to inadvertently spend that money.

In Texas and many other states, the state imposes a franchise tax. This is a very annoying tax that entrepreneurs often ignore. The problem with ignoring this tax for a corporation or limited liability company is the fact that your corporate charter will eventually be revoked. This can be devastating if a entrepreneur gets in trouble and needs to rely on the liability protection that a corporation or limited liability company normally provides. Suddenly, an entrepreneur may find himself personally liable for all the company debts simply because he didn't file this return and pay the tax.

Another problem is that the company will not be allowed to prosecute or defend itself in court if these taxes are not paid and the charter is allowed to be forfeited. This can be remedied simply by filing the return, paying the tax, and reinstating the charter, but many entrepreneurs don't know this and let creditors take default judgments against them at will. Fortunately, there are often exemptions, deductions or credits for small businesses that will eliminate or lighten the franchise tax liability for them. But for those who have to pay the franchise tax it will continue to be a problem.

Personal and real property taxes are almost always a line item in the bankruptcies I file. Since few taxing authorities vigorously prosecute those who don't pay them, they tend to be a low priority. Over time they can become quite large and difficult to pay. The best way to handle them is to establish an escrow fund. This can be done with the mortgage company or by creation of an escrow fund at a bank or savings and loan. Then each month you deposit one twelfth of the amount you will need for the year into a savings account. This can also be done for insurance too so that when the time comes to make the payment the money is in hand. Don't think you can pull these large payments from current cash flow. It just won't happen and you will just end up paying late fees and penalties.

I have had one entrepreneur, Dolly Templeton, in Chapter 13 for fifteen years simply because she didn't have the discipline to pay her property taxes. She bought and sold used household furniture and appliances and barely made enough to live. She had been married, widowed, and divorced several times and ended up with a home free and clear. Since there was no mortgage the taxes were not escrowed each month. When she failed to pay the taxes for three years, the City of Dallas turned her over to an attorney and a suit was filed. She didn't hire an attorney to contest the suit, so before long the property was put up for sale at a tax auction. With no money for rent, if she had lost her house she may have ended up on the street. That's when she sought our help.

We put her in Chapter 13 and were able to stop the sale of her home. The problem was that she now had to make monthly payments to the bankruptcy trustee. This didn't leave enough money left over for her to escrow taxes for the following year, so she was always getting behind on her payments. When she got too far behind, she'd get dismissed and we'd have to start over again. Unfortunately, repetitive bankruptcy filing is considered an abuse of the bankruptcy system, so two or three bankruptcy filings is the most anyone can hope to file. If our client lets this bankruptcy get dismissed, she will may end up homeless.

Dolly wasn't the only client with problems with property taxes. Another client, Charlie Jefferson, who owned dozens of low class rental properties in South Dallas, had a similar problem. Although he usually acquired his properties at a good price they often needed a lot of work to make them habitable. Since the county tax assessor-collector wasn't too diligent Charlie wouldn't worry about paying his property taxes. When they eventually got around to demanding he pay them he'd put one of the properties up for sale and catch up on all his taxes from the proceeds of the sale. Other than the interest and penalties he paid, it worked out pretty good until September 11, 2001 when the economy crashed and he couldn't readily sale or refinance any of his properties. Like Dolly he was forced into Chapter 13.

While an entrepreneur is in chapter 13 he is supposed to pay his current taxes as they come due or his plan can be dismissed. The tax collectors, however, often allow debtors to get behind again without reporting it to the Chapter 13 Trustee or filing a motion to dismiss. This is what happened with Charlie and Dolly, so when their Chapter 13 plans were over they were forced to immediately file another chapter 13 to pay out the taxes that should have been paying while in chapter 13.

Sales and use taxes aren't as much of a problem for the entrepreneur because a sales tax permit and a bond are usually required before a business can open. To get the permit, entrepreneurs are given instructions as to what is expected of them. The entrepreneur must remit the taxes periodically and, if they don't the taxing authorities come down on them quickly and effectively.

There are a myriad of other taxes and assessments state and local governments assess against the entrepreneur's property. Assessments for street improvements is one that can be quite devastating to the entrepreneur. When you buy real property, be sure and find out if the state, county, or city plans to widen the road in front of your property. These assessments can be very large and jeopardize the unsuspecting entrepreneur's ownership of the property should he be unable to pay it.

Finally, I have had many entrepreneurs devastated when they purchase or lease property and find out that, in order to get an occupancy permit they must make thousands of dollars of repairs. I know of several instances in which businesses that were planning to make a quick move to improve business or get a better lease rate, ended up out of business for several months while required repairs or upgrades were completed. Compliance with the American Disabilities Act, environmental laws and local codes and ordinances are usually the sources of these types of costly delays and business interruptions. If you have a realtor he or she should check all this out for you. If you don't use a realtor, you will have to do it yourself or hire an attorney to do it for you. But, whatever you do, don't ignore these most serious traps for the unwary.

15
When the Constable Knocks

When the constable knocks on the door, the natural inclination is to escape out the back door. Entrepreneurs seem to think that if they ignore a problem it will go away. This is not at all true. Problems need to be quickly identified and strategies developed to deal with them. When the constable comes by, invite him in and offer him a cup of coffee. After all, he is just the messenger and has no animosity towards you. You need to treat him nicely because if he ever comes by to execute on a judgment, you may need him to cut you some slack.

Lawsuits are usually long-term problems. They generally drag on for months or years. They're normally not an immediate threat to you if you hire an attorney immediately and answer the lawsuit. So, take the citation and call your attorney immediately. In Texas you have about three weeks to answer a lawsuit (the first Monday that comes after 20 days from date of service). This doesn't mean you have to actually go to court on this date, but simply that an answer must be filed before that date arrives.

If you don't file an answer, then a default judgment will be taken against you and, essentially the plaintiff will automatically get whatever relief he has asked for. Don't ever let this happen, get and attorney and answer the lawsuit. If you can't afford an attorney, you can answer the suit yourself, but the answer must be in writing and delivered to the court clerk. For a few bucks, the attorney you can't afford to have represent you might show you how to answer the suit Pro Se. Answering Pro Se is what it is called when an individual answers a lawsuit without an attorney. An individual always has the right to answer a lawsuit himself. If you are a corporation or partnership, you might have to get an attorney to answer. It is best to check with the individual court, as different courts have different rules.

If all else fails, go to the library or a bookstore and you can usually find a form book with the proper format for filing an answer. It's actually very simple. But get the lawsuit answered. Some people think just because the facts in the suit are a pack of lies that they don't have to worry about the lawsuit. This is not true. Those pack of lies will be considered the truth by the court if you don't answer the lawsuit!

After the lawsuit is answered, you will have some time to breathe. Litigation is a slow process, so use this breathing spell to find an attorney you can afford. Nobody likes to pay attorneys but sometimes you have to bite the bullet and get one. If you absolutely can't afford an attorney, call the local bar association and get a list of legal service agencies that provide services to the poor. If you are in business for yourself, this might be difficult as free legal services are designed for those without a job or any means of support.

Once the suit has been answered and you have an attorney articulating your position, you can relax. The vast majority of lawsuits settle and never go to court. This will probably happen in your case. Litigation is expensive and most plaintiffs don't want to bear the expense of litigating through trial. Settle your case and get it over with. It's better to pay out a little so you can refocus on operating your business.

If the lawsuit is one that can't be settled and threatens your ability to do business, then you may have to consider Chapter 13 or 11 to stay in business. Don't give up. There are almost always ways to get out of trouble. You just need to weigh your options with a good attorney and come up with a viable game plan. Many successful business owners have only achieved their success after failing more than once at making a business work. Often only experiencing defeat can make you wise enough and strong enough to be successful.

There are a few types of lawsuits that will require your immediate attention and response: garnishments, injunctions, attachments, receiverships, turnover actions, writs of sequestration, evictions, and executions. These are extraordinary legal maneuvers which can immediately threaten your ability to operate your business. An attorney must be immediately retained in these actions because they are highly complex and an individual without legal training couldn't possibly deal with them effectively.

A garnishment is the legal process where a creditor seizes one of your assets being held by a third party like a bank. The IRS uses this tactic a lot to take money from your bank account. This can be very disruptive because you usually don't know about the garnishment until after it has happened. By this time checks are bouncing and your business is in serious jeopardy. Garnishments can also be used to freeze assets that belong to you but others have in their possession. For instance, if a customer owes you money, your creditor could garnish that money, forcing your customer to pay that money to them rather than to you.

Injunctions also require your immediate attention and response because they are court orders prohibiting you from taking certain actions or requiring you to do something. They initially start out as temporary restraining orders (TROs), then may mature into a temporary injunction, and finally they may become a permanent injunction. If you don't pay attention to this type of court order, you can be found in contempt and fined or thrown in jail. The most common TROs that you will likely run into involve divorce actions. If a spouse of an entrepreneur decides to file divorce she will likely get a TRO that prohibits the entrepreneur from doing anything out of the ordinary course of business. If this happens, you need to consult an attorney immediately to be sure you don't violate the TRO.

TROs can also be used in conjunction with other lawsuits such as partnership dissolution. I have had several cases in which partners are disgruntled and want to prohibit other partners from using partnership money or from taking certain action. The courts will often issue a TRO to preserve the status quo and prevent any one partner from taking advantage of the other partners in breach of the partnership business.

Attachments, turnovers, and executions usually occur when a creditor gets a judgment against you. Once property of an entrepreneur is attached, control over that asset is gone. If you don't get an attorney's assistance immediately, you may lose that asset. If the attachment or execution is the result of a default judgment taken against you, you may be able to stop it by filing a motion for a new trial or putting up a bond while you appeal the judgment.

A writ of sequestration is an action to take possession of secured property. For instance an old client of mine, Monty Fillmore, utilized a lot of heavy equipment in his construction business. When the economy cratered in 2008 most new construction stopped in North Texas. Monty's business was okay until all his jobs were completed and he got his last retainage check. With no new business and employees who still needed to get paid, Monty got behind on one of his bank loans. The bank had all of his heavy equipment as collateral on the loan so when they got tired of waiting to get paid they demanded he surrender his collateral.

Monty, being a proud entrepreneur and good salesman, was negotiating on some new jobs and expecting at least one of them to come through. He couldn't afford to lose his heavy equipment so he hid them hoping to buy time until one of his new jobs came through. The bank didn't take too kindly to Monty's refusal to turn over the collateral so they filed a writ of sequestration to compel him to turn it over. At this stage the constable or a sheriff's deputy will usually come out looking for the equipment. If they find the equipment they will pick it up and take it back to be turned over to the creditor or sold to satisfy the judgment. If they can't find it the entrepreneur will likely be compelled to come to court and tell the judge where it is, so it's best just to turn over the equipment once you are cornered by the constable or a sheriff's deputy.

In Monty's case, however, the constable and sheriff couldn't find him or the equipment, so Monty kept it nearly six months before he finally gave up on getting any new jobs and told the constable where they could find it. Monty didn't tell me about the writ of sequestration because he knew I would have advised him to turn the equipment over. It's dangerous to try to avoid a court order by avoiding having it served on you. Courts don't take too kindly to that and there are criminal statutes that might come into play if an entrepreneur obstructs a creditor from obtaining his collateral.

Evictions obviously can't be ignored as if they are successful they will result in your business being shut down and your property either being seized by the landlord or dumped out in the street. In Texas evictions usually are brought in the justice of the peace court and even if you lose and are evicted the judge will usually give you time to get your furniture, inventory, and equipment out of the leasehold before the landlord is allowed to lock you out.

What you can't afford to do when you are sued is to sit around moaning and groaning about how you've been victimized by the legal system. You have to get an attorney and fight for your rights. If you don't, your creditors will win and you will be out of business. If you thought being a entrepreneur was going to be easy, well now you know that preconception was wrong. If you don't want to fight, then go to work for someone else.

Assuming you are in a normal lawsuit, once you have filed an answer, the discovery period commences.

This is basically a time when each party can require the other to provide information that might support their claims or defenses. This exchange of information is done by requests for disclosure, interrogatories, requests for admissions, deposition, and requests for production.

Most states have a pleading called request for disclosure which requires each party to disclose to each other certain basic information such as: the correct identity of the parties, who the witnesses are, what legal theories they plan to assert, and if they have obtained any witness statements. They have the same thing in federal courts called initial disclosures. This is information that the parties will almost always need, so the law requires they provide it automatically at the commencement of the case.

Interrogatories are used to obtain additional information not provided in the request for disclosure. Each side can ask each other questions which must be answered in writing under oath within 30 days. This is useful in getting specific information such as the identity and location of documents, dates, explanation of events, and background information on the parties.

Requests for production allow each party to require the other to let them look at all the records that might relate to the case. This is often critical to determine the facts necessary to prove a legal theory or defense. These documents must be produced and made available for copying by the other side so that each party will have time to analyze the documents and use them at the time of trial.

Depositions of parties and witnesses can be taken. This is a formal face to face confrontation in front of a court reporter, attorneys, and the parties involved. The witnesses appear by agreement or under subpoena. Witnesses can be made to bring documents by attaching a subpoena duces tecum specifying the items desired.

Finally, each side can send requests for admissions which are questions the opponent must either admit or deny. They are designed to save time at trial by determining uncontested issues in advance so the focus at the time of trial can be on the contested issues.

Once the discovery is complete, the court will usually order mediation or a settlement conference. This is a great time to settle your case and avoid a costly trial. A settlement conference is a gathering of the parties and their attorneys to try to resolve the case by agreement. A mediation differs in that an independent person called a mediator presides over a gathering of the parties and their attorneys to assist them in resolving the case. The mediation usually takes place at a neutral site and begins with an opening session. The purpose of the opening session is to allow the mediator to explain the process, have each attorney summarize their case, and then let the parties explain their positions.

This is the entrepreneur's opportunity to tell his opponent what he thinks about their case. It's a good time to vent and let out the frustration and anger that has been building up, so that meaningful negotiations can take place.

After the opening session, each party goes off to a separate room and the mediator shuffles back and forth taking offers of settlement between the parties. During this time the mediator points out strengths and weaknesses of each parties' case or defense and, hopefully, a settlement is finally reached.

It's important to have an open mind at mediation and negotiate in good faith. Remember anything can happen at trial. No matter how good a case is, it can be lost at trial and the entrepreneur can suffer a devastating blow to his small business. It's always better to stay out of the courthouse if at all possible and avoid any chance of total defeat. Remember you are a business owner and should be driven by the bottom line, not by emotions and pride.

If you don't settle and do end up in the courthouse, don't be surprised when your attorney wants a large retainer before the trial begins. The reason for this is that if you lose, your legal bill for the trial will be the last thing you ever want to pay. Remember your attorney is in business too, so he has to consider his bottom line just like you do.

Arbitration is another form of conflict resolution that you may run across as an entrepreneur. It will be represented to you as a stream-lined approach to handling business that is quicker and simpler than litigating in state or federal court. That is a lie. The problem with arbitration is it is very expensive for the parties involved. Not only do you have to pay for your attorney but you must also pay the cost of the arbitrator and the organization that is handling administration of the matter. Most entrepreneurs will have difficulty paying their own attorneys and cannot afford any additional financial burden. Our court systems are subsidized by the taxpayer so they are much more affordable for the average citizen. To make matters worse, even if you win in arbitration, you still have to go to a state or federal court to enforce the judgment!

Arbitration clauses are found in almost all commercial contracts because they benefit big business by taking the jury out of the picture. Big business believes it will fare better with an individual, retired judge, lawyer or businessman deciding their disputes with customers rather than a jury who may be more sympathetic to a small businessman. Banks, mortgage companies, landlords, and retailers all have arbitration law firms on retainer so they can afford the outrageous costs involved in arbitration but small businessmen cannot. My advice is to always avoid arbitration, if possible.

When an entrepreneur is reviewing a new lease or other contract, the first thing that should be stricken is the arbitration clause. I have found over the years that many landlords and even lenders are amenable to deleting it if you ask them to. I think they know it is unconscionable and feel guilty about it. The way I usually breach the topic is to say that I cannot recommend that my client give up his right to a jury trial. You won't always win the argument, but if you get into a serious dispute you'll be glad you pressed the issue and can litigate your case in state or federal court.

16
Bankruptcy, a Two Edged Sword

For the entrepreneur, a customer's bankruptcy can be devastating. Rarely is there a reserve for the loss of a large receivable. Even if it is a Chapter 11 or 13, which provides for the payment of a portion of the debt, it often takes months or years to actually receive any part of it. All the entrepreneur can do is file a proof of claim and wait. Occasionally, there are objections that can be filed and a bankruptcy attorney should always be consulted to see if there is any way to get the claim bumped up to secured or priority status. In some cases, it may be that the claim is non-dischargable. So don't give up. See a bankruptcy attorney and explore your options.

In many cases, the entrepreneur will have to file bankruptcy himself for his own protection. If he wants to stay in business, it will be a Chapter 11 or 13. If he wants to shut down the business or the business has no significant assets, a Chapter 7 might be appropriate.

Chapter 7 is designed to clean the slate and give the person filing a fresh start. To be eligible for bankruptcy, the entrepreneur must prove (1) he has more liabilities than assets, or (2) that he is unable to pay his debts as they become due. He also has to pass what is called the means test or prove that his debt is substantially business related. The means test is designed to make debtors pay part of their debt in a Chapter 13 if they can afford to. Basically. if the debtor's income, for the six months prior to filing, is less than the medium income for the county in which he lives considering the size of his family, then he can file Chapter 7. In most cases the entrepreneur will qualify for the business exception and not have to worry about the means test, but if for some reason he doesn't pass it immediately it usually will be just a matter of time until he does, since he's most likely unemployed.

If an entrepreneur qualifies for Chapter 7, he must surrender all his non-exempt property to the trustee appointed in the case. He is allowed to keep his exempt property such as automobiles, household furnishings, personal effects, qualified employee benefit accounts, life insurance policies, tools of the trade, and his homestead. He must choose between the state and federal exemptions which have significantly different provisions concerning what property can be kept. In Texas and Florida, the state exemptions are more favorable but, in certain cases, the federal exemptions may be appropriate. The bankruptcy attorney will help the entrepreneur decide the appropriate exemption election.

Getting a discharge is the main objective of a bankruptcy, as it is a release and forgiveness of most unsecured debts like credit cards, bank loans, and medical bills. After the discharge, creditors are prohibited from attempting to collect the discharged debts. Debts that may not be discharged are secured debts, priority debts such as taxes owed the government, unsecured student loans and domestic support obligations.

A secured creditor is the one who holds a

mortgage or lien on property owned by the entrepreneur. Secured claims only extend to the actual value of the collateral and the remainder of the debt is unsecured. Secured debts may be reaffirmed if the entrepreneur wants to keep the collateral, or surrendered if he does not. A reaffirmation is a new promise to pay a debt that would otherwise be discharged. Reaffirmations must be made before the discharge, must be in writing, may be revoked prior to entry of the discharge or within 60 days after it is made, and the court must approve them. An entrepreneur debtor has no obligation to reaffirm a debt.

A Chapter 13, sometimes called a "debtor adjustment," is designed to allow the entrepreneur debtor to reorganize his personal or business affairs. The objective is to allow the entrepreneur to keep certain assets in exchange for paying a portion of the debt that otherwise could have been discharged in Chapter 7. These payments are made to a trustee and extend over a period of three to five years. For the individual entrepreneur in trouble, a Chapter 13 may provide a way to save the business.

In Chapter 13, a plan is submitted for approval, called confirmation, which will provide for a monthly payment to be made to the standing Chapter 13 trustee. The Chapter 13 trustee distributes the plan payments to the creditors as set forth in the Chapter 13 plan and in accordance with the requirements of the bankruptcy code.

The amount of an entrepreneur's plan payment will depend on his income, allowable expenses, the amount of his debts, and the value of the assets he is retaining. He will have to prepare realistic personal and business expense budgets showing his expected income and expenses. The amount available after subtracting expenses from income is called the surplus which is available to make the plan payments. For a plan to be confirmed it must be feasible. For it to be feasible the surplus must be sufficient to pay the minimum plan payment required by the bankruptcy code. The plan payment must be paid for a minimum of three and maximum of five years. In most business cases the Chapter 13 plan will end up being five years since a significant dividend must be paid to allow the entrepreneur to retain his business assets.

Fewer objections are allowed in a Chapter 13 and some debts which would not be dischargable in Chapter 7 are discharged in Chapter 13. Most debts not paid through the chapter 13 plan will be discharged upon the completion of the plan. Secured debts will still have to be paid if the entrepreneur desires to keep the collateral.

If the entrepreneur's circumstances change during the course of the Chapter 13 case, they may be eligible to modify their plan to take these changes into consideration. For example, if one spouse loses a job, the plan may have to be modified to reduce the payments or suspend payments until the spouse gets a new job.

The entrepreneur debtor receives immediate relief from creditors the moment a bankruptcy is filed, as an automatic stay or court injunction takes effect that prohibits creditors from making contact with an entrepreneur or attempting to collect their debt.

To commence the bankruptcy process the entrepreneur debtor must obtain pre-bankruptcy counseling, complete and file schedules and a statement of financial affairs. The entrepreneur debtor will need to provide to his attorney the name and address of all his creditors and the balance owed to each, complete asset information, and copies of his last few years income tax returns. He will also be asked to prepare a budget of the entrepreneur debtor's monthly income and expenses.

Several weeks after the bankruptcy is filed, the entrepreneur debtor will have to attend a creditor's meeting before the trustee appointed in the case so he can determine if the bankruptcy paperwork is in order. At this time creditors can attend and ask questions. The entrepreneur debtor and his spouse, if married, must attend this meeting for the bankruptcy to be finalized. Before the case is over the debtor must take a financial management course and file a certificate of its completion with the court. Any reaffirmations entered into must also be filed and approved by the court before the case is closed out.

There is a downside to filing any kind of bankruptcy that the entrepreneur debtor must be aware of prior to filing. The most significant is the effect bankruptcy will have on his credit. A credit bureau can show a Chapter 13 on a credit report for seven years and a Chapter 7 for up to ten years from the date of filing. If the entrepreneur debtor's credit is already damaged, this might not matter. Or, if there is no other option, the loss of credit might be an acceptable risk.

Another drawback that entrepreneurs don't always understand is that in Chapter 7 they must surrender any non-exempt property such as investments, non-exempt real estate, and cash immediately after filing. In Chapter 13 they may be allowed to keep non-exempt property but they will have to pay additional monies into the plan equal to the value of the non-exempt property that they keep. The theory is that unsecured creditors should recover more from a Chapter 13 than a Chapter 7.

The trustee can make an entrepreneur debtor turn over assets acquired after the filing too, such as tax refunds, inheritances, insurance proceeds, lottery winnings, and other windfalls. The entrepreneur in Chapter 7 must report any such receipts to the trustee promptly so the he can decide whether to claim those assets or not. Large sums will always be taken, but many times smaller amounts will be abandoned by the trustee. In Chapter 13 the entrepreneur must amend his schedules and Chapter 13 plan to reflect the receipt of any subsequent receipts or windfalls.

Another risk in filing bankruptcy is the adverse publicity that often results. This is particularly bad for the entrepreneur debtor trying to reorganize a business. Sometimes sales will decline as some customers are scared off by the bankruptcy. Creditors who owe the entrepreneur-debtor money will suddenly get the idea they don't have to pay their debt because the business is in bankruptcy. This is a false, but common belief. The entrepreneur debtor will have to stay on top of his accounts receivable and advise anyone owing money that their obligation must be paid in a timely manner or it will be turned over to an attorney.

There are some debts that Chapter 7 will not discharge such as certain taxes, student loans, child support, alimony, intentional injuries to persons and property, and liability as a result of driving while intoxicated. If an entrepreneur debtor has any of these types of debts on the date of filing, he will have to arrange for payment of these debts outside the bankruptcy.

Secured debt, of course, is not discharged by a Chapter 7 or 13 bankruptcy, so the entrepreneur debtor will have to continue to pay such secured debts or surrender the collateral. If the collateral is surrendered, any deficiency will usually be discharged. Many times assets previously purchased are no longer needed in the business. Bankruptcy provides the option to surrender those assets to the creditor and get relief from that obligation. A similar provision applies to leases and contracts. This ability to pick and choose assets and debts to reaffirm is a critical tool for the entrepreneur debtor which often is the key to a successful reorganization.

Chapter 11 is another type of reorganization for individuals with larger estates, corporations, partnerships, and limited liability companies. It is dramatically different than chapter 13 in cost, procedure, and complexity. Whereas a Chapter 13 may only cost the entrepreneur $3,000 to $5,000, a Chapter 11 will be at least $10,000 to $20,000. A Chapter 13 is administered by the standing Chapter 13 trustee who takes care of much of the work that ordinarily would have to be done by the attorney. In a Chapter 11 the attorney has to do everything. Consequently, there will many more meetings with the attorney, hearings before the court, and administrative red tape in order to prosecute a case from start to finish.

Other differences include a much higher filing fee, the possible appointment of an unsecured creditors' committee, closer financial scrutiny by the U.S. Trustee's office, and the filing of a detailed disclosure document similar to what would be required in a stock offering. An accountant is almost always needed for financial reporting as well as assisting in proving the plan's feasibility including the preparation projections of how the plan will perform in the future.

One advantage to a Chapter 11 is that it has more flexibility. The term is not limited to five years as is the case in the Chapter 13, and the attorney can be much more creative in the specifics of the plan. Unlike a Chapter 13, the Chapter 11 plan will be put to a vote, so there is some politics involved.

There are some basic requirements for filing either a Chapter 11 or 13. Any debts owed at the time of filing must be listed on the debtor's schedules and cannot be paid during the plan without a court order. Debts and expenses incurred during chapter 13 or 11 must be kept current. Finally, the entrepreneur debtor is not allowed to get further in debt without permission of the court.

What this means is that the debtor must be able to operate at a profit immediately after filing bankruptcy. This is the downfall of most debtors. When they first file they don't always know what has gone wrong, so they don't know what adjustments need to be made to be profitable. Oftentimes, in months two or three of the bankruptcy, they will be already starting to get behind. In a Chapter 11 the U.S. Trustee's office monitors each debtor-in-possession carefully and, if they get behind on post-petition payments, the trustee assigned to the case is likely to file a motion to dismiss the case or convert it to Chapter 7.

Consequently, it's extremely important at the very

outset of a chapter 13 or 11 to identify what has caused the entrepreneur to be in the predicament he finds himself in and take swift, effective measures to resolve those issues. If the problem can't realistically be fixed, then a Chapter 7 should be filed and the business shut down. There's no point in prolonging the agony if the business can't be saved.

Bankruptcy is a very useful and powerful tool for the entrepreneur in trouble. Obviously, it should only be used if there is no other way out, but once it is invoked, it will likely be the best chance the entrepreneur has for survival.

17
Loan Consolidations and Workouts

Sometimes bankruptcy will not be a viable option for the entrepreneur for a number of reasons. A typical situation might be that the debtor has paid off a debt to a family member. If he files bankruptcy, the money that went to the family member might have to be returned to the debtor's estate as a preference. Let's say two brothers, Luke and Wally, are contractors. Luke is good with money and has accumulated a nice estate. Wally, on the other hand, spends everything he has and is always broke. Consequently, Wally is always borrowing from Luke. Despite Luke's help, Wally can't make ends meet and finally gets so far behind that bankruptcy seems like his only option.

The problem is: he had previously borrowed $140,000 from Luke and over the last year has paid him back $75,000 leaving a balance of $65,000. If he files bankruptcy, Luke loses $65,000, which he is prepared to write off because he loves his brother. But then his bankruptcy attorney tells him that not only will he lose $65,000, but he'll have to pay the bankruptcy trustee back the $75,000 that he received during the previous year.

Preference law is one of the most difficult legal principles to explain to entrepreneurs. What the law tries to accomplish is to put all creditors on an equal footing. Since family members have inside information and influence, it is common for them to be paid all, or at least some, of what is owed to them before the bankruptcy is filed. This would be unfair to general creditors, so the law states that anything received by an insider (family member, employee, partner, etc.) must be returned to the bankruptcy trustee to be distributed to general creditors in accordance with the priority system of the bankruptcy code.

A preference can also occur between unrelated creditors of the bankrupt debtor. The time is shortened from one year to 90 days, however. I recall one case in which a manufacturers' representative for a clothing manufacturer, Brandon, was owed commissions of about $60,000. This was the only company he represented, so he was very upset to learn his manufacturer was having financial difficulties. When he pressed the company for payment of his commissions, they put him off, but eventually gave him a check for $35,000, claiming there were some issues with the remaining balance due. Several weeks later the company filed bankruptcy.

Brandon was upset to have lost $25,000 but glad to get some money at least to tide him over until he found a new company to represent. Then one day he got a letter demanding that he return the $35,000 that had been paid him because it had been paid within 90 days of filing bankruptcy. Flabbergasted, he shot back a nasty letter to the bankruptcy trustee telling him that it was his money and he was keeping it.

It wasn't long after that he was served with a citation advising him that an adversary proceeding had been filed against him in a bankruptcy court in Maryland. At this point he conferred with a bankruptcy attorney and found out that he had to return the money unless he could come up a defense. Brandon had no defenses as the debt was long past due, but his attorney still haggled with the trustee and managed to settle the case for $20,000. Like anyone else, trustees don't like to litigate if they don't have to. It's expensive and often they have so many preference claims to handle it's not practical to litigate very many of them. So, even if an entrepreneur doesn't have a defense, a substantial discount may still be available if he stands his ground.

The best defense to a preference is that the debt was paid back in the ordinary course of business within the terms of the contract. I represented a computer consultant once who came to me with a preference letter wanting him to return his last check for $18,000. When I told him about the ordinary course of business defense he said he clearly fit within it. According to his contract he handled all of the company's IT and software maintenance. According to the contract he was to be paid in accordance with a formula every 60 days. He had a good relationship with the owner, so just hours before the bankruptcy filing he was cut his regular check which had just come due.

We answered the preference suit asserting the ordinary course of business defense. The trustee was not impressed at first but as we forwarded him documentation and showed him the client fit precisely within the defense he finally dismissed the preference action. A lot of times trustees send out preference letters to everyone who got a check within 90 days of filing bankruptcy without any real investigation taking place, so it's imperative to get a commercial bankruptcy attorney involved right away to see if a defense might be available.

So, if an entrepreneur has paid a preference to someone and he doesn't want the recipient of the money to have to return it, bankruptcy will not be an option until the preference period has gone by. Another reason he might not want to file is if he has personally guaranteed so much of the debt that filing a bankruptcy will not really be of much help to him personally. Just as soon as the corporation files Chapter 11, the creditors will start coming straight to him, so if he files bankruptcy for the company he will have to file personal bankruptcy as well.

Another alternative to bankruptcy is the workout. What this involves is negotiating with creditors to get them to take less than what is owed to them. For instance, if $100,000 is due to creditors, the debtor might propose a workout of $25,000, or 25 cents on the dollar. Whether or not creditors will accept a workout depends on whether they can be convinced that it is the best deal they can get. For instance, I often tell creditors that they can either accept 25% now or chance getting zero if a bankruptcy is filed. Some will tell me to take a hike, but most will reluctantly accept the lesser amount because, as a practical matter, it is very difficult to collect from a creditor in trouble. This is particularly true if the debtor is out of state.

Sometimes workouts take months or years to accomplish, as some creditors will resist the workout and file suit to collect the entire amount. Others will simply just stubbornly refuse to agree to anything less than the full amount. Over time most will succumb and accept the amount offered. The ones who hold out will either end up getting paid in full or get nothing.

In one instance I contacted a creditor of a florist I was doing a workout for and offered $18,000, which was 50% of what was owed. The creditor was very hostile and told me his attorney would be calling me back. The attorney was equally belligerent and asked if I would accept service for my client. Over the next nine months while we were litigating this case, all the funds we had for the workout were exhausted. Eventually, the hostile creditor got tired of the expense and hassle of litigation and offered to take the $18,000. We politely informed him that there were no longer any funds available for settlement.

In another case the opposite happened. The creditor jumped right in and filed suit. He prosecuted the suit vigorously and would have jeopardized the entire workout had we not settled with him. In this case he finally accepted an 80% payout, which was much higher than anyone else received, but a necessary concession under the circumstances.

The entrepreneur must be careful, however, when it comes to workouts. There are a lot of scam artists out there who promise that they can settle debts for ten cents on the dollar if you will just pay them a fee or a percentage of what you save from their efforts. Unfortunately, I have known many entrepreneurs who have paid thousands of dollars to these type of con artist, most of which went into their pocket. Using a reputable attorney, who has to answer to a bar association if he does anything unethical, is your best bet if you want to do a workout.

A bill consolidation loan is a new loan obtained for the purpose of paying off several existing debts with the net result usually being a longer payout at a lower interest rate. In this case if the entrepreneur has $30,000 in credit card debt at 21% interest and is paying the 2% minimum monthly payment of $600. If he only pays the minimum payment each month he may never get the loan paid off. So he goes and gets a loan for $30,000 at 10% interest payable in 15 years. His monthly payment is now only $322 which improves his cash flow dramatically.

Whether the entrepreneur can get a loan for either of these purposes will depend on several factors whether or not: (1) his credit is still good enough, (2) he has collateral for a loan, or (3) he can get a co-signer. One common source of funds for a workout is home equity. Lenders love it because they can have a fully secured loan and, if the debtor defaults, there is usually enough equity in the property to be assured of a full recovery. Home equity loans, however, should be avoided, if possible, as the home that is paid off or has small mortgage payments can provide the entrepreneur much needed security in an otherwise hostile environment. Knowing that even if the business fails he won't be out on the street will give him much confidence and peace of mind.

Another common way to get loan consolidation or workout funding is with a loan guaranteed by someone with good credit or someone who has collateral to pledge. Friends, family members, or partners are usually good sources for this type of help. In one case a contractor, Peter Walker, was very popular and always busy.

Unfortunately, he didn't know how to run his construction business and got farther and farther behind on his payroll taxes, until the IRS was about ready to shut him down. Since payroll taxes are not dischargable in bankruptcy, a workout was his best option.

In this case Peter teamed up with a friend, Tom Banks, who knew how to run a business but knew nothing about building a house. Tom loaned him the money to pay the IRS with the promise that they would do future business together: Tom running the new venture and Peter handling operations. Thus bankruptcy was avoided and a new enterprise was begun that probably had a much better chance of survival than Peter had as a sole proprietor.

My standard advice to clients is, if possible, stay out of court. Once you surrender yourself to the jurisdiction of the courts, then you have lost control over your life and must accept whatever judgment the court imposes. So, if it isn't absolutely necessary to file a bankruptcy, then a workout is the best way to go. Often you can accomplish nearly as much on your own without giving a judge control over your destiny.

18
Employees, Double Trouble

Good employees are critical to the success of any small business. The owner usually can't do everything himself, although some owners try. It's important to find employees who are capable, dependable, and have a good, positive attitude. But often that is a very long and time-consuming process, which few employers have the time or patience to perform consistently. Consequently, the process is often short-circuited, resulting in substandard employees and performance.

In my own situation, finding good employees has been one of my most difficult tasks. Good legal secretaries and paralegals command high salaries. In my early years of practice, I couldn't afford an experienced paralegal or even a top notch legal secretary. As a result I had to hire inexperienced secretaries and train them. This wasn't a very efficient way to operate, as I was forced to spend my valuable time training employees and forced to do trivial work that they should have been doing.

It was all a matter of confidence. Since they were not knowledgeable and well trained I lacked confidence in them and was afraid to turn tasks over to them that I had no business doing myself. This resulted in low productivity and the necessity for working long hours to make up for it. After a while I got used to doing everything myself and forgot the importance of delegating. To make matters worse, about the time I'd get a secretary or paralegal trained and finally felt confident delegating meaningful work to them, they'd get lured away by a big firm who could pay a much larger salary.

Once I got my practice established and could afford to pay a competitive salary, I discovered another problem. It isn't always easy to find competent employees. Prospective employees tend to exaggerate their experience and training. Few small business owners have the time or patience to thoroughly test employees to verify their skill level. Nor do they bother to verify resumes. It's human nature to trust people and to believe what they tell you. Unfortunately, in today's world, this is a very perilous practice.

The process of screening and selecting employees can be delegated to professionals or employees trained specifically to perform that task. However, this can be very expensive, and there is no guarantee that the employee placed with your company will be any better than someone you personally hand picked.

Once you select and hire an employee, you then face a whole host of other issues such as payroll, health insurance, sick time, vacation pay, workman's compensation, and retirement. All of these are highly complex issues which few entrepreneurs enjoy dealing with, yet failing to effectively deal with any one of them could be fatal to a small business.

Other minefields are discrimination in employment because of sex, age, race, religion or national origin, and the American Disabilities Act. In Texas an employee can normally be terminated my his employer at any time and for any reason unless (1) they are protected by the federal civil rights statutes, the US Constitution or Bill of Rights, (2) state laws that make it illegal to terminated someone if they refuse to break the law, and (3) state laws making it illegal to terminate someone who has filed or is about to file a workman's compensation claim. What this means to the entrepreneur is that he must be very careful not to break any of these laws or suffer serious consequences.

I have received many calls from entrepreneurs over the years seeking advice as to how to fire an employee. I always ask them if the employee to be terminated is in a class that may be protected like being female, over forty, sick, disabled, or a from a minority race or religion. This is often the case so I caution them that they must be very careful in the manner in which these employees are fired. First, they must document carefully the reason for the termination and gather credible evidence to back them up. Secondly, they must be sure there hasn't been a trend of terminating persons in any of these protected classes. Thirdly, they must confront the employee and make sure they are aware of the deficiency in their performance. Finally, unless it is a very serious offense, they should put them on probation first and give them an opportunity to conform their behavior to acceptable standards.

Entrepreneurs are often upset that they can't just fire an employee on the spot, but I caution them not to do that unless the offense is something intolerable or dangerous such as theft, fraud, reckless endangerment, coming to work under the influence of drugs or alcohol, and sexual harassment.

What I often advise my client is that rather than firing an employee it's better to let them quit. Over the years I have found that once an employer makes it clear that the employee's behavior is unacceptable and puts them on probation, the employee becomes uncomfortable and soon will quit. This is the optimal way to end a relationship with an employee. I often recommend that the employer encourage bad employees to quit by offering them small severance packages like several weeks or months of severance pay and continued health insurance during that period. The severance package, of course, will be conditioned on the employee signing a general release of all potential civil rights or other employment claims under state or federal law.

Entrepreneurs often balk at this and are so angry they don't want the offending employee to get another dime from them, but I point out even having to defend a frivolous discrimination claim will be far more expensive than just working out an amicable termination of the employee. The smart entrepreneur will put his emotions aside and take this advice.

For an entrepreneur many of these issues can be handled by others. A payroll service can be employed to handle payroll, human resources, workman's compensation, payroll taxes, and health insurance. A good insurance agent will do the paperwork for all your casualty insurance needs. An actuary or brokerage house can handle your pension or 401K needs. It's important that the entrepreneur is not distracted by these types of administrative quagmires. Delegate them to other employees and professionals who are trained to handle them. Just be careful in the selection process. Get a referral from someone who has used them in the past and is very satisfied with their performance. Beware of second-hand and "brother-in-law" referrals, in which the person giving the referral has no personal knowledge of the professional's competence.

PART III -TURNING IT AROUND

19
Getting an Attorney

Once the business is stabilized, then all attention must be turned to making it profitable. Whatever mistakes have been made in the past must be identified and eliminated. To do this, an attorney, accountant, and possibly a business consultant will be needed. Think of your small business as a small kingdom at war. You are surrounded by armies ready to attack at any moment. They have one objective, and that is to take everything you own at any cost. Your attorney is the commander of your army—the army who will defend you while you're trying to rebuild your kingdom which holds all your worldly possessions. Pick your commander carefully, as his or her skill will be critical to your survival—and for godsakes, pay him so he won't abandon you.

It amazes me how entrepreneurs in desperate trouble treat their attorneys. Often their bills are neglected or ignored altogether when they are in the heat of battle. The entrepreneur often treats the attorney like he is just another creditor, expecting him to work without being paid. But few attorneys will put up with this and, if you run up a big bill with your attorney, you'll soon find yourself with a new, more dangerous creditor at your heels demanding payment. So remember, if you don't pay your army, they will neglect or abandon you, and always at a time when you can least afford to be defenseless.

If your attorney is so critical to your survival, how do you find the best one for the job? Usually, the best way is by referral. But only accept a referral from someone who has used the referred attorney in a similar situation. Many people refer an attorney they know nothing about. They may have seen him on TV, heard his ad on the radio, or found out about him from a friend or relative. Every week I get similar referrals of clients from people who don't know me. While I appreciate these referrals, you're not doing anyone a favor if you refer them to someone you know nothing about.

It is also important that the referred attorney is experienced in the area for which you are seeking representation. A friend might refer you an attorney who did a great job handling his divorce, but that same attorney is not likely to be the best person to guide you through a successful reorganization of your small business.

If you can't get a referral from someone who has successfully reorganized their business, then you may have to turn to a referral service. The local bar association is probably the best, but you still must be selective. The bar associations do not screen the attorneys who they recommend. Usually, the criteria is simply that they are licensed to practice law, are a member of their association, and have malpractice insurance. You need to interview the attorney referred to you to be sure he or she is experienced in helping a small business under siege. The sure test of the attorney's ability is to ask the attorney for references from three small business owners who he has successfully reorganized. If he can't or won't provide those references, keep looking.

Once you have found the right attorney, confess to him all your sins. Be honest and tell him everything that might impact the defense of your business. Everything you tell your attorney is confidential, so don't be timid, shy, or too embarrassed to tell all. The worst thing for an attorney is to be blind-sided at trial or in a hearing. On one occasion I was helping a middle-aged woman shut down her failed business. It appeared to be a simple Chapter 7 bankruptcy, but she seemed to be a little more nervous than expected. I quizzed her about it and she said it was just her nature. At the creditors' meeting, her nervousness increased, and during my questioning she suddenly confessed to having $25,000 in cash stuffed under her mattress.

Of course, I was flabbergasted and greatly disturbed, because failing to disclose assets in a bankruptcy is a criminal offense. Fortunately, I was able to convince the trustee that the woman simply thought because the money wasn't in her checking account, she didn't have to report it. This is a common misconception of debtors. They think that by giving cash or property away to a friend or relative, they don't have to report it on their bankruptcy. My client was lucky she didn't end up in jail.

The sad thing is she lost $25,000 that she probably could have kept had she been honest with me. If I had known she had $25,000 we probably could have figured out how to legally keep it or spend it prior to filing bankruptcy. Since she wasn't honest with me, she lost the money and nearly ended up in jail.

Many states have so-called board certified attorneys who have special training in a particular area of law practice. Whereas a board certified bankruptcy attorney may be excellent at getting you through bankruptcy, he may know nothing about the proper structure of your business, minimizing estate taxes, or handling employee issues. A general practitioner, who is a small businessman himself, may actually be better than the bankruptcy specialist.

Sometimes you will need more than one attorney to get you through the problems you face. In one instance we were representing a client who was having financial difficulties due to an automobile accident. He had been cut off by a large truck and suffered a severe concussion that left him with brain damage. He could still function, but lost the ability to run his business. In this case, we were able to handle his personal injury claim and file a Chapter 13 bankruptcy to try to preserve his business until he could recover, but we were not competent to handle a Social Security disability claim. We, therefore, referred him to an attorney who specialized in Social Security disability and monitored that case closely while we prosecuted the other actions. If you need more than one attorney, hire them, but select just one to be in charge of all the others so he can coordinate your legal affairs during this critical reorganization period.

Once you have one or more attorneys, keep in touch with them. Be sure you advise them immediately of any communications from creditors or new circumstances that could impact your reorganization. Your attorneys should promptly return telephone calls, but if they don't, be persistent and don't give up until you have reached them. Attorneys are busy and often take too long to return phone calls. If you can't get through immediately to the attorney, talk to his secretary or legal assistant. They are usually much easier to contact and will have direct access to the attorney.

If communication with an attorney becomes too difficult or impossible, then hire a new one. You have the right to hire and fire your attorney at will, so don't be afraid to do so if necessary. This may be your one chance to get your business back on track, so don't let a bad choice of an attorney keep you from attaining your goal. Remember it is your future that is at stake, so take charge of the situation and do what it takes to be successful.

20
Form of Business

One of the first decisions that will have to be made during the reorganization process is what type of entity will best suit your business. Most small businesses come to me as sole proprietorships. This rarely is the optimal form of a business as it is important to keep the individual and business separated for efficiency and protection of personal assets. Usually a limited liability company, corporation, or limited partnership is what is needed.

A corporation has traditionally been the vehicle of choice for small businesses. It is a distinct entity, which is itself a taxpayer. It provides centralized management, liability protection to its stockholders, and free transferability of interests. It is well understood and recognized as the normal way to do business in America.

A limited liability company is a more recent breed of business entity, but it is rapidly becoming the obvious choice for the entrepreneur. It provides the same centralized management, free transferability of interest, and liability protection, but has the option of being taxed itself or being taxed like a partnership. Normally, the entrepreneur will elect to be taxed like a partnership so the profit and loss of the business will pass through to the owner directly. This eliminates any possibility of having profits taxed as a dividend and allows the entrepreneur to use business losses to offset other personal income.

There is one drawback for an individual entrepreneur setting up his business as a limited liability company. IRS may consider it a sole proprietorship and make him file the business on Schedule C of Form 1040 rather than a separate partnership income tax return. This doesn't help in keeping an entrepreneur's business and personal lives separate which is a big problem with entrepreneurs. So, it may be better for a single entrepreneur to be a Sub-S corporation rather than a limited liability company.

Occasionally a limited partnership will be the vehicle of choice if there are investors who want to put money in the business, but do not want operational responsibility. Limited partnerships can often provide tax advantages and other advantages that a corporation or limited liability company cannot. Therefore it is important to look closely at the business with your accountant and attorney and determine which type of organization is best for you.

Once the choice has been made a conversion must take place. This can be a fairly complicated process that must be done very carefully to avoid adverse tax consequences. If a conversion is not possible, sometimes the best approach is to shut down the old business and start over in a new business vehicle. Either way, it is important to get this done quickly, as the business vehicle in which you operate is the foundation upon which you will build your newly restructured business, and you want it to be strong and durable.

21
Accounting and Bookkeeping

For many entrepreneurs, accounting and bookkeeping are their nemeses. Entrepreneurs usually believe they can handle their own bookkeeping and rarely have a professional do it. Consequently, very little bookkeeping actually takes place until an accountant is finally hired to prepare a tax return a year later. By this time the bookkeeping is of no value to the entrepreneur as it is water under the bridge, and it may be too late to rectify the situation. To make matters worse, critical records may have been lost, which may make it impossible to create an accurate set of books.

In this day and age, when we have easy accessibility to computers, there is no excuse for not keeping a good set of books. When I first started my law practice in the 70s, reconciling my bank statement was a difficult and time-consuming task that took hours. Bookkeeping had to be delegated to an accountant or bookkeeping service, as there simply wasn't time to run a business and keep accurate books. Usually, by the time the bookkeeper provided financial reports, it was too late for them to be of any value in avoiding cash flow problems.

With the advent of computers, many programs were developed to assist bookkeepers with their tedious job. These programs, however, were difficult to learn and often temperamental. I remember cursing the ones I used on a regular basis and wondering if they actually saved any time. They did save time though, because they eliminated the need for doing any kind of math, which I've found many entrepreneurs avoid at any cost.

Then there was Quicken®, and I thought God had shined down on all of us. It was so simple and made bookkeeping so easy that I quickly began pulling my financial reports every morning. If anything didn't look right, I could immediately get to the bottom of it.

So, today when you can write a check and do your bookkeeping at the same time with Quicken® or Quickbooks® or one of many other bookkeeping programs, every entrepreneur has the ability to effortlessly keep an accurate set of books and can pull up a financial report instantaneously. This is a tremendous tool for the entrepreneur and solves one of his greatest problems. Yet many entrepreneurs still don't keep books and still operate their businesses in the dark. This is just crazy.

I don't know if they are lazy, scared of new technology, or afraid to face the truth about their business. They say ignorance is bliss, but the entrepreneur's bliss will be short-lived as the fabric of the business begins to give way. It is imperative that entrepreneurs get on top of their bookkeeping. This used to be a problem; today it is easy. If you are not doing bookkeeping, stop what you're doing right now, and go buy a bookkeeping program that does your bookkeeping every time you write a check. Then spend a day or a week, if that's what it takes to learn the program, and your bookkeeping problems will be over. Don't ever write a manual check again!

Once you learn the program and know how to pull up the reports you will need from time to time, you can delegate the actual bookkeeping to someone else and get back to whatever aspect of your small business you do best. But get the program and learn how to use it properly, and you will be well on the way to making your small business prosper.

Another related issue is record keeping. Very frequently I will represent entrepreneurs who are being audited by the IRS. If the truth were known, they would owe no taxes, but unfortunately they quite often have not kept records of their income and expenses, so when they are asked to prove the deductions they have taken they are out of luck. Every year thousands of entrepreneurs pay hundreds of thousands of dollars in taxes they don't owe, simply because they were too lazy to get receipts, keep their invoices, and retain their bank statements.

In an audit, if you can't prove your deductions, the IRS will disallow them. Conversely they will charge the entrepreneur with income for every dollar that shows up as a deposit even if, in reality, the deposit is a redeposit or transfer of money already considered as income. If you can't prove the source of the deposit, it will be considered income and you may end up paying taxes on it twice.

Avoiding overpayment of your taxes, however, is not the only reason entrepreneurs should keep all their records. Records are needed in litigation if you are trying to prove a claim against someone, or defending a claim asserted against you. Years ago, our firm contacted all of our clients to see if they took the diet drug Fen-Phen. For those who had taken the drug for six months or more, it was likely they would be entitled to $500,000 in compensatory damages. All they had to do was produce doctor or prescription records showing that they used the drug for this period. Unfortunately, most of those who were eligible to recover this money didn't have any records to substantiate their claim. Instead, they had to hope the pharmacy or doctor had the records. Many people did not recover a dime even though they took the drug for the minimum period. This was a shame and could easily have been avoided.

Record keeping can be very time consuming and tedious work if you do a good job of it. But record keeping doesn't have to be all that organized to be effective. Sure, it would be best if you kept a file for every creditor, supplier, customer, and employee, and stored them neatly in a file cabinet, but that isn't absolutely necessary. Today, everything can be easily scanned and stored on a hard drive or in the cloud. Ideally, it should be stored in a searchable format for easy access. The key factor is that the record must be kept for later retrieval. If scanning isn't practical, all you need is a banker box. When a bill is paid, a bank statement reconciled or correspondence received, simply throw it in the box. When the box gets full, seal it up, date it, and get a new box. Continue to throw all your receipts, invoices, check registers, and any other written records in your storage box instead of the trash can.

Down the road if you have an audit or need to prove a claim, you search your hard drive or go to the storage box and find what you need. It will be a lot of work sorting through a box of records, so I would suggest you throw your records into the box in alphabetical order. This can be done by simply putting in a divider for each letter in the alphabet and taking just a second to throw them into the right letter. This will make later retrieval much easier. So from now on, don't throw away business receipts. Simply scan them or throw them in a storage box and forget about them.

Even with a good accounting program, you'll still need an accountant to do your taxes. But the cost of the accountant will be much less, because they won't have to do a year's worth of accounting before they can do the tax return. If you are reorganizing your business, it is of critical importance that you hire an accountant to do your bookkeeping and to prepare monthly financial reports to provide to the court.

With the help of an accountant, the entrepreneur can monitor the progress in turning the businesses around. If the turnaround is not going well, the entrepreneur and the accountant together can figure out what further adjustments are needed to make it work. Trying to reorganize a business without accurate financial statements is like trying to ride a bucking bronco blindfolded—a rather futile and perilous undertaking. And doing it without professional help is foolish and shortsighted.

Hiring an accountant is a little different than hiring an attorney. Most accounting firms will have the expertise to do your accounting and tax preparation. What you need to look for in an accountant is whether he is strictly a numbers man, or will he be able to give you practical advice in structuring and running your business? Will he simply be an agent for the IRS, or will he be on the lookout for ways to reduce your taxes?

Once your accountant has been selected, he needs to help you prepare a realistic budget and provide you with monthly financial reports so you can see if you are keeping within your budget goals. Sadly, few entrepreneurs see monthly financial reports, and fewer yet ever get around to doing a budget. Yet, to successfully reorganize, these types of reports must be prepared religiously and studied carefully as soon as they come out.

Many entrepreneurs will not understand the financial statements that their accountants produce. Part of the accountant's job is to teach the entrepreneur what the balance sheet and income statement mean. If you don't understand the reports your bookkeeper or accountant has prepared, ask questions and keep asking questions until you do understand. If the monthly financial statements show that you are not meeting your budget goals, ask your accountant what you can do to get in line with your budget. If the problem is beyond his expertise, you may need to hire a business consultant.

Again, you have to be careful in the selection of a business consultant. Don't ever hire the one your banker or other secured creditor refers to you. He or she may be a spy for the creditor whose objective is to squeeze as much cash out of you as they can before you go under.

Business consultants can be found at colleges and universities, in the yellow pages, on the internet, or in business journals. Try to find one with experience in your industry, if possible. The consultant's goal should be to help you with marketing and business operations that are outside the scope of your attorney's and accountant's expertise.

Business consultants often must literally go to work for the entrepreneur for a time to really get a handle on the business and its challenges. Usually they are much less expensive than the accountant or attorney, so it is practical to have them for ten or twenty hours a week if need be. They can train the entrepreneur in proper business practices, bookkeeping, budgeting, and marketing. They can train employees and help the entrepreneur find customers and vendors that will help ensure successful operations in the future.

In a recent case, an entrepreneur died and left his lucrative real estate business to his two sons. Fortunately, one of the sons worked in the business but, even so, his father handled most of the critical operations, so neither had the expertise to keep the business going. When the father had come to me for estate planning he told me his sons would need help when he died and asked me to make sure they got it. I told him that would be difficult as I could give them advice but couldn't guarantee they would take it.

The solution we finally arrived at was to set up a trust, appoint the two sons and myself as co-trustees. This way they would have to consider my advice and only if they both agreed could they disregard it. As it turned out the two sons were very suspicious of each other. Roger, who had worked in the business was resentful that his father had given his brother, Paul, half of the business and Paul was fearful that somehow his brother would take advantage of him due to his superior knowledge of the business.

Because I was a trustee and had no allegiance to

either brother they both more or less trusted me and we were able to work through most of the issues that came up. As it turned out their father had left a lot of loose ends that none of us had the expertise to resolve, so we called in a business consultant to help get the business under control, and then to teach the sons how to successfully run it. After six months, not only was the business still around, it was thriving and even operating more efficiently than when their father had been in charge.

22
Changing Your Ways

Once you hire your accountant it's important to do a budget to determine what cutbacks to make. Frequently there will have to be layoffs, salary reductions, and suspensions of fringe benefits. Rent may be too high, which will require re-negotiations with the landlord, or termination of leases and executory contracts in bankruptcy.

If the entrepreneur has been looting the company, that has to come to a halt. If the company has too many employees or simply can't afford what it has, the whole operation of the business will need to be reviewed to determine how labor can be better utilized so that fewer employees will be required.

If payroll taxes haven't been paid and proper procedures for collecting and paying these taxes aren't in place, that situation needs to be corrected immediately. It's not wise to finance your reorganization with Uncle Sam's money. It's an expensive loan, and one that will only cause you immeasurable grief in the long run.

This is a critical stage in the reorganization process and must be done as quickly as possible, for there has to be a certain amount of cash available to continue operations. If the negative cash flow isn't stopped quickly enough, the business may run out of money and be unable to reorganize at all.

Too often entrepreneurs wait too long to seek legal counsel and the business is too far gone to be saved. It is important to be realistic and seek help at the first sign of trouble. This is another reason an ongoing relationship with an attorney is important. If the company has an attorney that it deals with on a regular basis, it is more likely the entrepreneur will pick up the phone as soon as bad fortune rears its ugly head.

This is the time to take a good look at insurance too. Many entrepreneurs operate without insurance. They think that insurance is a luxury that they will get down the road when they have extra money. Well, if you want to build a successful business, you have to realize a lot of things will go wrong and prepare for those eventualities. If you want to roll the dice and go naked you can, but only at your own peril.

The wise entrepreneur will find a good insurance agent and sit down and figure out what insurance is absolutely necessary and get it in force immediately. In my experience, an entrepreneur should have personal life insurance as well as disability, medical insurance, business interruption, automobile, general liability, workman's compensation, fire, and extended coverage on his real estate and contents insurance. Additionally, it is wise to get a blanket umbrella liability insurance policy, both personally and for your business.

This sounds like a lot, but if you shop carefully you can often get these casualty type coverages included in a single policy, which will be much cheaper. Personal life insurance, disability and medical coverage can often be purchased with your group insurance, which is also a lot less expensive than if you purchase each individually.

A good insurance agent can handle all your insurance needs and take care of most of the onerous paperwork involved. It's a good idea to find an agent who is willing to take this burden off your shoulders and handle claims too, so that you won't be saddled with this task or have to pay an employee to handle it for you.

I had the same insurance agent for twenty-five years and, whenever an issue came up, I made one phone call and it was resolved. Conversely, if my agent became aware of industry changes or issues that I should know about, he called me immediately. If I missed a premium, he would give me a personal phone call to remind me to pay. Unfortunately my agent died so I had to shop around for someone to replace him. It took a while to find someone as good, but I eventually did. If you have five different insurance agents, you won't be a big enough client to warrant special attention and you won't get the kind of service you need.

I can't tell you how many times I have been forced to defend clients who thought they had insurance but for some reason hadn't paid the premium. Sometimes they were short on funds, but often it was as simple as forgetting to send in a change of address or the insurance notice getting lost in the mail. Defending a lawsuit can cost thousands of precious dollars that few entrepreneurs can afford. If the lawsuit is lost, the business may be forced into bankruptcy or put out of business.

Insurance is not a luxury. It is a fundamental requirement for anyone who operates a business. Just as a policeman wouldn't go into a crack house without a bulletproof vest, neither should the entrepreneur pass another day without adequate insurance to protect him from the perils of doing business.

23
Funding the Turnaround

If you can avoid having to get additional financing for your business, you should do so. Loans are easy to get but hard to pay back. Unfortunately, some entrepreneurs will have to find financing to turn around their businesses. Certain businesses require maintenance of large inventories, expensive equipment, or large quantities of supplies and materials that the entrepreneur may not have the capital to purchase. This will necessitate procuring short term credit to finance these items. Unfortunately, an entrepreneur trying to turn around a failing business is not likely to have the credit to get this type of financing.

A common source of this type of funding is the entrepreneur's current secured lenders. Although the entrepreneur's credit will probably be pretty bad, his creditors may be willing to loan additional funds because they don't want to have to deal with a non-performing loan if the entrepreneur's business fails. A loan default can cause them considerable problems with bank examiners, stockholders, or investors. As a result, they will often be willing to provide additional capital, provided there is sufficient collateral to cover the new advances, and prospects for a turnaround are good.

This type of financing, however, often comes with strings. The bank will be keeping a very close eye on the entrepreneur's activities while it is funding the turnaround. It will also be expensive funding, as the bank will require a higher interest rate and a quicker payout due to the higher risks associated with the loan. You will no doubt have to personally guarantee the loan, pledge your ownership interest in the business, assign your life insurance, and bow down before your loan officer whenever you see him.

If your existing lenders are not interested in advancing more funds, other possibilities include finding new investors, joint venturing projects, asset sales, and home equity loans. Of all these options, getting new investors is the best, of course, as no payback would be required.

Home equity loans are also attractive because the payback is stretched out over time. It's important, though, not to undertake a home equity loan unless you are absolutely sure that the turnaround will be successful. Often the equity in a entrepreneur's home is the only asset he has. Since homesteads are exempt property it would be a shame to give up this last asset and then not successfully reorganize.

Sometimes when a small business downsizes it will have assets it no longer needs. These assets can be sold to fund future operations. Another way to acquire assets needed for business operations is through joint ventures with other companies. For instance, I previously mentioned my builder client who was good at building, but couldn't handle money and had no credit. So when he wanted to start a new house, he joint ventured the project with his brother. The brother handled all the financing as his contribution to the partnership and my client built the house.

In another case of mine, an entrepreneur was a distributor of specialized truck parts. Normally he would get orders for a part, buy the needed part, and then sell it to the customer. Unfortunately, after he filed his Chapter 13, he didn't have cash to buy the parts for resale. So what he did was get another company to buy the part, sell it to him at a little markup, and then he'd resell it to his customer. Since nobody knew who the ultimate customer was, this worked pretty well. The joint venture partner had very little risk as he usually bought on credit and was paid by my client before he had to pay the supplier.

If none of these sources of financing are available, some clients have turned to high interest lenders, some legal and some not. I have had clients who had loans with interest rates as high as 900% per annum. Some small lenders who make very high risk loans are allowed to charge this type of interest, but usually when you see these loan shark interest rates, the loans are not legal.

In Texas the most an unlicensed lender can charge varies from 18% to 28% percent, depending on the prime rate at the time. Other states have similar laws. Lenders get around this by setting up complicated factoring arrangements or inventory purchase agreements. A few years ago a client brought me one of these contracts. The way this one worked was that a lender purchased an inventory item from my client, who was a manufacturer. He then sold it at a premium to my client's customer. Theoretically, there wasn't a loan—just a purchase and sale, but actually the entire transaction was handled by the manufacturer just as if the lender wasn't involved. When I put the pencil to it, the cost to the manufacturer was the equivalent of a loan at seventy-two percent per annum.

These quasi-usurious loans should be avoided at all cost. Should you be so desperate that you need to resort to this type of lending, odds are you are not going to be successful at reorganizing. Since these loans almost always require personal guarantees and collateral assignments of your interests in the business, it is usually financial suicide to enter into them. Additionally, the people who make these kinds of loans are often shady at best, and may resort to violence should you default. So, stay clear of this type of illegal lending.

For the entrepreneur trying to reorganize, additional debt can be very burdensome and may jeopardize his ability to successfully turn his business around. Think very carefully about whether new debt is absolutely necessary. Sure it would make things easier, but can you survive without it. If you can, then don't borrow more money. Bite the bullet and do without the new cash. In the long run, you'll be glad you did.

24
Restoring Your Credit

If an entrepreneur finds it necessary to file a Chapter 7, 11, or 13 it will be important to reestablish good credit as soon as possible once he receives his discharge. Many people think filing bankruptcy will permanently destroy a person's credit, but that isn't true for two reasons. First, a person's credit score will usually rebound quickly as he now has no debt and all the individual negatives have been consolidated into one blemish–a bankruptcy filing. Secondly, since so many people are filing bankruptcy these days and lending is so lucrative, creditors can't resist exploiting such a large market. Accordingly, filing bankruptcy isn't as much of a blemish on your record as it was in years past.

Unfortunately, an entrepreneur's credit may not come back by itself because many creditors intentionally misreport their customer's credit after filing bankruptcy and some will even continue trying to collect the discharged debt. You would think there would be someone in the government making sure creditors obeyed the bankruptcy discharge injunction and the Fair Credit Reporting Act (FCRA), but that's not generally the case. That task is largely left to the individuals themselves, which means most often nothing is done and the predatory creditor is allowed to continue to ruin the lives of its victims.

Fortunately, there are a myriad of laws available to stop this type of abuse by the credit industry. The first is a contempt action in the bankruptcy court, the second are federal actions under the Fair Credit Reporting Act (FCRA) and the Fair Debt Collection Practices Act (FDCPA), and the third are state court actions for unfair debt collection, defamation, unreasonable collection and invasion of privacy.

Unfortunately, these laws are not utilized often enough to completely stop this type of abuse. Two of the reasons are consumer's ignorance of their rights and their residual guilt for filing bankruptcy. Even if they know their rights have been violated, they are not inclined to take action against the lender who was forced to write off their debt. What they don't know is that their creditors haven't necessarily given up getting paid and sometimes won't quit until forced to do so.

Since an improvement in the entrepreneur's credit will only happen if the old creditors properly report his credit, it's important for the entrepreneur to check his credit after bankruptcy to be sure his debt are listed as "discharged in bankruptcy" and show the balance to be "zero." If this isn't the case, in addition to the adverse impact of the bankruptcy, all of the old blemishes that should have been removed will continue to pull down his credit score. An entrepreneur can dispute adverse credit himself, but often creditors don't correct the adverse reporting even after it is pointed out to them. If creditors refuse to report a consumer's credit correctly after bankruptcy it's important to seek legal help to make them obey the law. This shouldn't cost the entrepreneur in the long run as the law provides that attorney's fees are recoverable if it becomes necessary to sue a creditor to force compliance with the credit laws.

Another problem is creditors simply ignoring the bankruptcy. We all know that when a debt is discharged in bankruptcy that's the end of it, right? Think again. Creditors have a sack full of tricks to get consumers to pay debts that they don't have any legal obligation to pay. In fact, there is an entire industry of debt buyers out there that most people don't even know exist. I'm not talking about the collection agencies, but companies and trusts that do nothing but buy and sell debt—some of it already discharged. Obviously, if they are buying the debt they intend to collect it. Below are a few of the ways it's done.

When the bankruptcy is over the entrepreneur will eventually need to finance new equipment, obtain a lease, get a line of credit or finance a new car or home. When he goes to apply for a loan the loan officer will pull his credit and may tell him that he doesn't qualify—unless he can pull up his credit score a few points. They suggest he contact some of his creditors who are negatively reporting their accounts on his credit report and settle the debt. He protests that the debt has been discharged but they just shrug. So, he takes their advice, contacts the creditors and pays off some of the discharged debt. What he wasn't told was the negative reporting should not have been on his credit report in the first place.

Several months after the bankruptcy discharge comes through, an entrepreneur may start receiving telephone calls or letters from a company he doesn't recognize. He thinks perhaps he forgot to list the creditor on his bankruptcy schedules and he is still liable for the debt or the collector says this debt isn't discharged by the bankruptcy. It gets ugly from there and the entrepreneur ends up settling with them. What they don't tell him is that they bought the debt from a creditor who was listed in the bankruptcy or that, in a no-asset-case an unlisted debt is still discharged.

After the bankruptcy is over the entrepreneur continues to pay an auto loan or home mortgage, although he doesn't formally reaffirm that debt. Later on, he gets behind on the payments and the car is repossessed or the house foreclosed. Months later, a collection agency comes along and tries to collect the deficiency. They tell him since he continued to pay on the debt after the bankruptcy was over, he has waived the discharge. What they don't tell him is that the debt is still discharged and usually not collectible. The creditor's sole remedy, in most cases, is to take back their collateral and that's it.

Finally, after the bankruptcy is filed, some of the entrepreneur's creditors will quit updating his credit report so they don't have to report that their debt has been discharged. They hope he will voluntarily pay them later to improve his credit score. What he is not told is that this trick called "parking an account" and he can dispute the account and make the creditor update it without paying them a nickel.

After the bankruptcy is over there are ways to improve his credit score. If the entrepreneur has an auto or home loan that he has reaffirmed, he won't need to apply for a credit card to reestablish his credit. Just paying these bills on time is all he needs to worry about. If he is still paying on a car or home loan but didn't reaffirm the debt the creditor may not be reporting to the credit bureaus, so his credit won't bounce back the way it should. Sometimes he can get these creditors to begin reporting again, but he will have to contact their bankruptcy department and ask them to start reporting. They will probably need him to sign a waiver since reporting a discharged debt would be a discharge violation. Because of this, some creditors will still refuse to report current house or car payments to the bureaus even if a waiver is offered. But it won't hurt to try.

If an entrepreneur has no open credit accounts that are reporting to the bureaus after the discharge, he may want to apply for an auto loan or credit card so he can start building his credit again. If he does, though, he should be sure he can afford it. If he hasn't already done a family budget he should do it now.

To do a budget he should follow these steps:

(1) write down the families' net income (after taxes and deductions)

(2) Make a list of all the families' expenses each month including the cash that is spent. Be realistic. Then add it up and subtract it from the income.

(3) If there is a surplus, then it would be prudent to apply for a credit card or auto loan as long as the minimum payments are less than the surplus amount.

(4) If there are more expenses than income forget about obtaining new credit.

The entrepreneur should only get a new credit card or auto loan if he can easily make the minimum payments each month. If he misses payments, his credit score will go down instead of up. If he gets a new credit card, he should put the card on automatic pay from a checking account for the minimum payment due each month. When the paper credit card bill comes in, he should pay as much more as he can by check. Don't ever max out a credit card. Borrow less than one half of the credit limit. Try to pay the full balance when the bill comes at least once or twice a year. Only use the credit card for emergencies or to cover short term shortfalls. Don't ever apply for a new credit card to provide cash to make payments on another credit card. Finally, the entrepreneur should avoid adding family members as authorized users of a credit card as multiple cards are much more difficult to manage.

The entrepreneur should review his credit reports annually. This may seem obvious, but most consumers don't look at their credit reports until they are declined for credit or are alerted by a third party of a problem. Instead of waiting be proactive. Consumers can go to http://annualcreditreport.com each year and get a FREE copy of their credit reports from Experian, Equifax, and TransUnion. Be sure and download the reports in PDF format so they will save to your computer for later reference

Be sure and dispute all reporting errors that are discovered. It does no good to review credit reports if the errors are not disputed. Unsecured debts that were included in the bankruptcy should be reported as "included in bankruptcy," "Chapter 7 or 13 Bankruptcy" or "Wage Earner Plan." If the bankruptcy isn't mentioned the reporting should be disputed. Debts included in a bankruptcy that were discharged should have a -0- balance. If they show a balance owing, then the account should be disputed. Debts included and discharged in a bankruptcy should have no other derogatory statements in the "Status" line other than the bankruptcy notation. If the status line includes things like "collection account," "past due," or "charge off" it should be disputed. The reason that should be given to justify the dispute is that it can't be a collection account because the creditor can't try to collect it, it can't be past due because nothing is owed, and it can't be a charge off unless it was reported as a charge off before the bankruptcy was filed. If it is reported as a charge off after the bankruptcy is filed, it would be a stay or discharge violation.

If an entrepreneur has forgotten to list a creditor in his bankruptcy he should immediately send the creditor a copy of his discharge by certified mail. There is case law in some jurisdictions that holds that in a Chapter 7 no-asset-case, the unlisted unsecured debt is still discharged. So, give the creditor 60 days after a copy of the discharge is sent and if the reporting is not corrected, dispute it. If the creditor doesn't respond within 30 days, the reporting should be removed. If the creditor responds and confirms the reporting then a consumer attorney should be retained to help get it removed.

Debts incurred after the bankruptcy was filed won't be discharged, but these trade lines can still be disputed if they are reported incorrectly. If an account is not recognized, the amount is incorrect, or there is something else wrong with the way it is being reported it should be disputed.

If an entrepreneur is in Chapter 13 each credit line included in the bankruptcy should show a status of "Chapter 13" or "Wage Earner Plan" with the current balance due on the debt after any payments made by the

Chapter 13 Trustee. In Chapter 13 when a plan is confirmed all defaults are cured so there should be no other negative remarks in the status line such as "collection account," past due" or "charge off." If there are, dispute them.

In Chapter 13 cases review all credit reports again 3-6 months after the discharge to make sure the discharge is reported correctly. Review the credit reports carefully. Don't just glance at the reports looking only for the obvious errors. Check the individual's names listed and make sure they are all correct. If a name listed was never used, dispute the listing. Also, look at the addresses where they claim the entrepreneur has lived. If he didn't live at any of the addresses listed, dispute the listing.

Check the reporting of each creditor who claims you have an account with them. If you don't have an account with them, dispute that listing. When checking a credit line make sure the amount is in the ballpark. It will never be exact, but if it is way off, dispute it. Look at credit inquiries section carefully. Regular inquiries (hard pulls) should only be made if a consumer applied for credit. Account reviews inquiries (soft pulls) should only be made if the consumer has an open account with the creditor. If the debt has been discharged the creditor shouldn't be doing account reviews.

We all witnessed lender greed and corporate excess during the 2008 economic meltdown and its aftermath. Entrepreneurs should not feel guilty about enforcing their discharge injunction or utilizing other state and federal laws to protect their fresh start. Congress enacted the bankruptcy laws to give individuals and entrepreneurs a second chance because people make mistakes or are victims of forces over which they have no control and it is better to focus on the future rather be paralyzed by the past.

The Lawyer's Lament

The dreaded call deep in the night
A plea for aid that can't wait for light
Torn between duty and sloth
The good lawyer rises like a moth
Fluttering off to do his tedious job
Of defending some poor slob
Who probably won't ever pay his bill
Nor even thank him for his skill
In springing him from that sleazy jail
The check? Oh, it's in the mail.

25
Mind, Body and Spirit

One of the keys to the successful operation of a business is taking control of your physical and emotional health. This is even more important if you are trying to turn around a failing business. If you are not feeling well, you may not have the necessary focus and energy to make the drastic changes that are needed to insure success. Every business owner gets depressed from time to time, but the owner who is facing a possible business failure will face an unbearable emotional strain. Worry, embarrassment, anger, frustration, fear—these emotions will become so overwhelming at times that the entrepreneur will likely become irritable, short-tempered and depressed. To cope with these emotions the entrepreneur may turn to snack foods, tobacco, alcohol, and drugs. I know this to be true because I have suffered through depression myself as a small business owner. Many times I have been on the brink of financial disaster and felt overwhelmed.

For the first twenty-five years of my practice I ate too much, got very little exercise, and had a difficult time sleeping. Consequently, I was forty-five pounds overweight and suffered from the usual list of ailments such as acid reflux, irritable bowel syndrome, headaches, muscle spasms, back pain, aching teeth, and insomnia. It wasn't until I got my last child through college and felt a little financial relief that I finally became proactive about my health.

I knew I couldn't do it on my own, so I convinced my wife to go on the Atkins Diet with me. It was from that diet I learned the importance of purging my diet of excessive sugar. This wasn't easy for me as I had a sweet tooth. I loved cookies, pies, candy, soft drinks and always put three sugars in my coffee. The thought of avoiding sugar seemed impossible. Luckily, it didn't take long before I started feeling much better and for the first time since I was a child didn't have to take antacids every night. We lasted on that diet about six months and both lost about 10 pounds before we abandoned it, but we continued to avoid sugar and were healthier for it.

Several years later we tried the Nutrisystems Diet and each managed to lose about another ten pounds. From it I realized two things: the importance of controlling the quantity of food you ate and the value of eating five times a day rather than the traditional three meals. Over the years I had tried many diets with little success. My metabolism was so slow even if I reduced my calorie intake significantly, I still wouldn't lose any weight. It was very frustrating. So, I was shocked after switching to a five meal a day regiment that I finally started losing weight. The smaller, more frequent eating caused my stomach to shrink and my metabolism to increase.

The introduction of the Fitbit watch, however, is what really got me on the right track. In the past when I started any diet the first instructions were to make sure to get plenty of exercise, drink lots of water, eat right, and get lots of sleep. I usually skipped over these steps because they were just common sense, nothing new, and

I thought I was doing fine in those areas. I was wrong, however, but had no way of knowing it. But when I got my Fitbit, for the first time I had a way to measure all those things every diet guru agreed was fundamentally important. Now, I could easily keep track of my diet, steps, and sleep habits and I was shocked to realize how poorly I was doing in those areas. Of course, now there is the Apple Watch and other similar devices that are just as effective.

Armed with the knowledge the Fitbit provided me, I was able to finally develop and maintain an effective diet and exercise routine. As a result, I began to gradually lose weight until I got down to my target weight of 185. While this was happening, I ran across one of Dr. Steven Gundry's infomercials about certain common foods we ate that inhibited proper digestion. I'm not going to go into all of his theories but what I realized from his message was the need to take plenty of probiotics to replenish our stomach's supply of good bacteria.

My wife was a nurse and studied nutrition when she was young, and she always blamed our obesity on my dislike of vegetables. How could she prepare a nutritious meal without vegetables? I didn't argue with her because there were quite a few vegetables I didn't like and they seemed to be her favorites. But there were also many vegetables I liked or could tolerate, but not cooked. For some reason I prefer vegetables raw. But, the truth was neither of us really appreciated how our diet was adversely impacting our lives.

In my research I found the experts agreed that a nutritious diet would consist of approximately 60% carbohydrates, 25% protein and 15% fat. So, now with the help of my Fitbit, I was able to formulate my own diet of foods that I liked but foods that were also providing the right balance of carbs, protein and fat. Because I enjoyed all that I was eating, it was no problem staying on my diet and everything I needed was at my local supermarket. So, for the last several years I have been able to maintain my weight for the first time in my life and all the health issues I had endured for so many years went away.

The Fitbit for the first time allowed me to monitor my sleep. In the past I simply calculated the time I went to bed against the time I woke up to determine how much sleep I was getting. I quickly learned with Fitbit, however, that just being in bed doesn't mean you are sleeping. There are sleep stages four sleep stages, awake, light sleep, deep sleep, and rem. The Fitbit records each of these stages so you know if you are getting not only enough sleep but the right kind of sleep.

Finally, the Fitbit allowed me to monitor my physical activity. Being an attorney and writer my life is very sedimentary. Most of the day and night I'm sitting behind my computer. My fingers are getting a lot of exercise, but that's about it. The only exercise I got on a regular basis was climbing stairs. I knew exercise was important, but being an entrepreneur and a workaholic I didn't think I had time for it. My office was in a high rise, so I did get into a habit of climbing the stairs rather than taking the elevator. This was good but not enough, so I started walking and set a daily goal of 11,000 steps. It was hard to make the time for walking. The only thing that made sense was to walk at lunch, so that's what I do now. To make it more enjoyable I listen to music or audio books while I walk. This makes the time go more quickly.

When the weather is bad I walk in the mall but if it is nice out I go to a nearby park and walk the trails. Just to round out my exercise plan I do some simple yoga exercises when I first get up in the morning and, after work I stop by the local recreation center and swim 8-10 laps in the pool. All this exercise takes only an hour and a half each day and has improved my health immeasurably.

So, every entrepreneur should develop their own individual diet, sleep and exercise plan that works for them so they won't be debilitated by all the ailments that poor eating habits can cause. Because, even if they are in good health keeping a small business running smoothly will not be easy and there will always be a lot of stress. The source of most of the stress in my life was poor cash flow. My problem was I didn't know how to turn down a case. I wanted to help everyone who walked through the door and never thought about whether they could pay me or not. Even when they didn't pay, I hardly ever withdrew from a case. It just felt wrong to abandon someone in trouble.

Consequently I've written off hundreds of thousands of dollars in fees and expenses over the years. You would think doing that would gain me some goodwill with my clients and it usually did, but not always. I remember a single mother, Amanda, who came in when her home was about to be foreclosed. She was supposed to pay me $500 a month toward my fees and expenses while I prosecuted a lawsuit against her mortgage company. She made the first payment but that was it.

The lawsuit dragged on for over eighteen months but I managed to keep her and her daughter in their home that entire time without her making a single mortgage payment. Finally, we settled the case on a very favorable basis. The mortgage company agreeing to re-amortize the loan to cure the default, paying me about half of my actual attorney's fees and deleting any adverse credit on her credit reports. At first Amanda was elated with the outcome of the litigation but after a few days she became bitter that I was getting the only cash out of the settlement. I pointed out that I was writing off half of what she actually owed me, but it made no difference to her. In the end she said I was just another greedy lawyer. Her words hurt a lot and made we wonder why I had ever taken her case. For weeks I was depressed and had trouble concentrating on my other cases. Fortunately, my disappointment paled in comparison to what I saw some of my clients going through, so I got over it.

When I first started law practice, I got a call from a woman whose husband had committed suicide. He had a small vacuum cleaner business that hadn't been doing so well and he had become very depressed. One day his wife came home and found him dead—a self-inflicted gunshot wound to the head.

As I got into the case, I discovered that the business had some financial problems, but nothing so bad that it couldn't have been fixed. In fact, the wife's brother took over the business and we were able to successfully reorganize it under Chapter 11. As I worked on the case, I felt very sad to think that a young man took his life needlessly and for something as unimportant as money.

Too many of my clients over the years have turned to drugs and alcohol as an escape from their stressful lives. This only makes matters worse and leads to other, more serious problems. In recent years I have seen two clients literally destroy their lives using illegal drugs. One committed suicide and the other one has been teetering on the brink of a mental breakdown.

Because of these sad experiences, I have made it a personal goal to help my clients avoid this type of tragedy. Some attorneys, when they meet a client with financial troubles, are very negative and often chastise their clients for their stupidity. This is an intentional tactic designed to make the client so fearful that they will immediately do whatever the attorney asks and pay whatever he charges. This is despicable behavior and it sickens me when I see it or hear about it.

The first thing I try to do with a client is to assure him that it isn't the end of the world. Although the situation may seem bleak, the fact is there are a lots of ways to successfully reorganize a business and I am sure we will be able to come up with a viable strategy. Then I remind them that money isn't what is important in life. It is their friends and family that matter and as long as they have those things, they are blessed. I tell them to quit worrying about their creditors as I would be taking that burden off their shoulders. They usually leave my office very much relieved and they usually tell me so.

To successfully reorganize your business, you must be optimistic about the future. A good attorney will do his best to make you feel this way, but often that won't be enough. Things will go wrong, creditors won't always cooperate, and doubts and anxieties are bound to creep back into your mind. There are several ways to deal with fear and depression while you are trying to turn around your business. A technique that worked for me in the early years when money was tight was to work overtime.

Rather than sit at home worrying about work, I set up an office at home, and at 6:00 or 7:00 every night, I shifted my work from the office to home. By working 60 hours a week, I actually felt better because I was earning more money and directly attacking the source of my anxiety—my work. This is not the ideal solution, and it has made me a workaholic over the years, but it is better than going to a bar or to the racetrack. When money is in short supply and labor expensive, oftentimes the entrepreneur must work long hours and wear several hats to survive.

Another technique is diversion. Over the years, spending time with my wife and children was always a great diversion. When times got particularly stressful, we'd go fishing or travel. I was always able to forget about work when I was out on the road or out at the lake. After the kids grew up, I took up writing as a diversion from my stressful law practice. This has worked well and helped me maintain my sanity during some pretty tough times.

There are hundreds of other types of diversions that can help reduce stress, such as hunting, fishing, hiking, skiing, scuba diving, hockey, basketball, football, baseball, and tennis. Participating in these activities not only helps you forget about your problems, but also keeps you in better physical condition, which, in itself, helps your ability to cope with stress. Even if you don't directly participate in a sport, just being a spectator can be very beneficial by allowing you to escape into another world and forget about your troubles. One of my sons plays video games to escape and I know many people escape into their smart phones. Entrepreneurs should find a hobby, a sport, or other activity that they enjoy and pursue it with great enthusiasm. They all need the ability to relax, recharge their spirit and clear their minds of worry and anxiety so that when they come to work each day, they are ready to tackle the difficult tasks that await them.

26
Succession Planning

Once a business has been successfully turned around and is profitable, it is time to think about the future. Although the owners will probably want to operate the business for a long time, at some point one or more of the principals will quit working, become disabled or die. Dealing with this eventuality is called succession planning. Unfortunately, few small business owners give it must thought until it is too late.

Nobody likes to think about discord, disability, or dying but these things happen. The most common problem is discord. One or more of the owners becomes unhappy about how the business is being operated, profit splits, or some other issue and wants to sell his interest or buy out his partners. If this issue hasn't been addressed and agreed upon in advance the future of the business may be jeopardized.

Invariably, the disgruntled owner will think his ownership interest is worth far more than what his co-owners are willing to pay. But even if they can come to an agreement on the price, few small business owners will have the cash to buy out a co-owner. So, if an agreement can't be reached, the alternative is liquidation of the business and the pro-rata distribution of the proceeds to the owners. Of course, this would be a tragic end for a business that had almost failed but had been turned around and made profitable.

The way to avoid this problem is to negotiate and fund a buy-sell or stock redemption agreement when the business is formed or when it becomes profitable. The way a buy-sell agreement works is the owners agree that in the event one of them quits, becomes permanently disabled, divorced, or dies, the remaining owners can buy his interest at an agreed price or by utilizing an agreed formula for calculating the price. A redemption plan is different in that the business buys the seller's interest rather than the owners. To make sure the owners have the money to honor such agreements, the owners or company can buy life and disability insurance to fund them. And, if one of the owners wants to quit and sell his shares, the agreement can provide the sale of his interest at the same agreed rate but with a long-term payout that the remaining owners can afford from the profits of the business.

The attorney who sets up the entrepreneur's business can easily draft a buy-sell or redemption agreement, but if the owners can't afford this legal expense, most insurance companies who sell the insurance to fund these agreements have excellent forms that can be easily edited to fit any business situation.

Another issue that will come up once a business becomes profitable is high taxation. As the owners' tax brackets increase they are going to want to find ways to decrease their tax liability. One of those ways is to set up a retirement plan for the owners and employees. Retirement plans are expensive to fund and administer but they provide significant tax savings to the owners while providing critical retirement income. The downside is the necessity to include employees and comply with ERISA non-discrimination rules.

Every profitable business should set up a 401K, pension or profit sharing plan, but it is something that should be considered very carefully and monitored closely. It is also wise to hire an expert administrator, CPA or actuary to handle the onerous reporting and compliance issues. This is not something the average entrepreneur is going to want to deal with. Many of the major brokerage firms offer pre-approved plans that they will administer free if the fund invests its money with them. These arrangements are often the best solution for the small business owner who isn't going to have the time or expertise to handle the day to day administration of a retirement plan.

Profit sharing plans are usually better for the entrepreneur in the beginning because they don't have to be funded if there are no profits. Stay away from defined benefit plans that require contributions every year whether the business has a profit or not. 401K plans are very popular too, but be careful of any mandatory contributions by the employer each year. There are lots of options, just be sure the business will have enough profit to easily make any required contributions.

PART IV - CASE STUDIES

So far we've talked a lot about problems that face small business owners. I've told you some stories from my experience over the years in helping entrepreneurs, but in order to really understand the process of defending a entrepreneur I want to take you through some fictional example from start to finish. While the following names and events are not real, they are inspired by actual cases.

Case Study 1
Greenbrier Cleaners

Don Parker and his wife Louise came to see me one afternoon after they had been sued by their landlord. My receptionist showed them into my office. Don, a tall robust man wearing glasses, looked to be in his late 50s and his slim, attractive wife in her mid 40s. They were both stiff, somber and subdued when they took a seat across from me.

"So, you own a dry cleaners," I asked to get the conversation going.

Louise nodded. "Yes, we inherited it last year."

"Was this your first venture into the business?"

"Yes and no. My father owned a dry cleaning business when I was young. I worked part time at his plant while I was going through school."

"So, you liked the business?"

"No. Not really. It wasn't a very glamourous life. My father wanted me to work in the business after I graduated from high school but I wanted no part of it. "

"So, how did you end up in the business?"

"Well, I went to Richland College and when I graduated I was able to get a good secretarial job at TI. That's where I met Don. He was a ceramic engineer at the time and we fell in love and got married. We worked almost ten years side by side at TI until my father recently died."

"Oh, I'm sorry to hear that."

"Well, it actually came at a good time as Don was laid off about the same time."

"Oh, I see. You inherited the dry cleaning business from your father."

"Exactly. My only sibling was a brother in Des Moines and there was no way he was coming back to Dallas to run a business, so my father left it to me."

"Okay. So, what's the lawsuit all about?"

Don sighed. "I don't know if you are familiar with a dry cleaning operation, but one of the pieces of equipment we have to have is a boiler."

"Right. That makes sense."

"Well, the boiler has a vent that goes through the roof to the outside."

"Uh huh."

"Unbeknownst to us there was a leak in the vent and the hot, moist air that usually was vented outside instead went into the attic of the shopping center for God knows how long—months, I'm sure. Anyway, over time the moisture compromised the roof support beams and eventually the roof collapsed."

"Oh, my God!"

"We have insurance but, wouldn't you know, there is an exclusion for leaks in pipes."

"What? That's ridiculous," I said.

Don raised his eyebrows. "That was our reaction too, but our insurance agent says the exclusion is quite clear."

"Hmm. I'll have to take a look at your policy."

Louise handed me a copy of the policy. It was thick and printed in small print. I scanned through the policy and found a paragraph on exceptions. Sure enough the exclusions was right there.

"I can't believe they would put a clause like this in a boiler policy. I don't suppose your agent explained these exclusions to you?"

"No. Not at all. He just wrote the policy and took our money."

"Okay, so the landlord is suing you for the damage to the shopping center roof."

"Right," Don confirmed. "$125,000 in damages so they say."

"Damn. That's a lot of damage."

"So, needless to say we don't have that kind of money," Don said dejectedly.

As I pondered the lawsuit and the insurance policy my heart sank. It looked like an impossible situation. Defending the lawsuit would be difficult and expensive and the best we could hope for would be to settle for something less than what the landlord was demanding.

"Well, we need to answer the lawsuit and file a cross-action against the insurance company. It will be a battle of the experts to determine what caused the roof damage. It's possible something else was responsible for the damages. You never know. Anyway, that will buy us some time at the very least."

"How much will that cost us for you to defend us?" Louise asked.

"Well, it won't be cheap. Litigation can get rather expensive. I'll need $5,000 up front and before you're done you could spent $20-$30,000 with no guarantee as to the outcome. A lot depends on how vigorously the plaintiff prosecutes the case and how much effort you want to expend defending yourself."

"What do you think our chances are if we try to defend ourselves?" Louise asked.

"I can't say for sure, but honestly I don't feel all that optimistic about it. I'll have to study the insurance policy some more to see if there is any way around the exclusion, but on the surface it looks pretty clear. Do you have any cash available to offer a settlement. It may be best not to waste a lot of money defending the case, but rather try to settle as cheaply as possible before everyone runs up their legal bills."

"We don't have any spare cash. We need ever dime we have just to keep the doors open."

"What other debts do you have," I asked wondering if they were a candidate for some sort of reorganization. If the business was struggling that might be the best way to handle the landlord's lawsuit. A chapter 13 or 11 would stop the lawsuit in its tracts and allow them to pay all or a portion of the debt over a three to five year period.

"We had to assume a note to the bank for $90,000 and there is a $36,000 line of credit with Chase Business Card. Regular monthly payables are about $12,000 and we are a month behind on our lease."

"What about personally?" I asked

Louise sighed. "Well, we have about thirty-five thousand in credit card debt, two auto loans and the home mortgage."

"What we may want to explore is a chapter 13 or 11. We don't want to sink all your money into the roof problem and end up losing the entire business. Tell me about the assets of the business."

"Ah. Well, we have equipment and leasehold fixtures with a cost value of $120,000, inventory of maybe $20,000, a delivery trucks worth $30,000 and cash and accounts receivable of $10,000. We also had to assume a shopping center lease of $3,600 per month. Of course, we have our customer list. It has about 1,800 names, addresses, and telephone numbers of the customers within five square miles of our location.

"Who does the bookkeeping?" I asked.

"I do," Louise replied, but I'm afraid I've been so busy lately that we are a tad bit behind."

"So, let's say you weren't facing this problem with the landlord and the roof. Do you think you would be able to survive?" I asked.

"Well," Don replied thoughtfully. "During the first ninety days after we took over the business it lost over $10,000. I had to borrow $4,000 on our Visa card to make ends meet. With this cash we were able to survive two more weeks when, fortunately, business began to improve. We barely made payroll on the fifteenth, but managed to squeak by. Since then business has gotten back to normal and we have managed to at least break even."

"Well, I think your best bet is to file a chapter 13. It's the cheapest way to handle the lawsuit and it will also allow you to improve your cash flow."

"How will it do that?" Don asked warily.

"Well, since you have been forced to personally guarantee all of the business debt you can include it in a chapter 13 along with your personal obligations and pay it out over five years including your car loans, credit cards, medical bills, delinquent rent. Then you will just have one payment each month to the chapter 13 trustee."

"I seriously doubt our creditors will go along with that?" Louise noted bitterly.

"They won't have any choice in the matter. As long as you comply with all the chapter 13 rules the creditors won't have anything to say about it."

"What about the bank?"

"As long as the bank's note is due in less than five years, it can be added too."

Don thought a moment. "I believe its $2,000 a month with a balloon after three years."

"Well, that's a disaster just waiting to happen," I advised. "If the bank refused to renew the note you'd be out of business. With the chapter 13 you'll be able to pay it out over 60 months and know at the end it will be completely paid off."

"Won't our monthly payment be astronomical," Louise asked skeptically.

"It will seem high but if you compare it to what you were paying before I think you'll find it will be substantially less. The only thing I'm worried about is if the landlord asserts a claim for the roof. Theoretically in a chapter 13 when you are keeping the business, you would have to propose a 100% plan. If the landlord were to assert their claim in the bankruptcy court and it were allowed you would have to pay it along with the rest of your debts over five years. Of course, if you had to do that the business couldn't support the plan payment each month."

"So, what do we do if that happens?" Don asked.

"Well, we will list the claim as disputed and unliquidated. That will put the ball in the landlord's court. If he files a proof claim asserting a deficiency we would object to it. That would mean they'd have to spend a lot of money fighting us and they might not want to do that knowing they'd still have to wait years to get paid. But, if they went through all that and prevailed, we'd either have to convert to Chapter 11 or Chapter 7. If it were a Chapter 7 you would lose the business. If it were a Chapter 11 we could propose a plan that only paid ten to twenty-five percent on the dollar which you could no doubt afford."

"So, why don't we just do a Chapter 11 from the beginning?" Don asked.

"Because a Chapter 11 is much more complicated and expensive. You'd end up paying twenty-five thousand dollars in attorney fees and it could take eighteen months to get approved. A Chapter 13 is simple and straight forward. I think it would be best for you if the landlord will cooperate."

"What do you think the chances are that they will?" Louise asked.

"Pretty good, actually. I'm sure they have secondary insurance that will kick in if you don't pay. A lot of time insurance company's don't want to get involved in a bankruptcy proceeding that will stretch out for years. Let's just hope that is the case with your claim."

When they left my office they were leaning toward the chapter 13 but had to think about it. I told them they needed to do a budget to make sure after we filed their bankruptcy that the business could support the chapter 13 plan.

Several days later they faxed me a budget. They estimated sales to be about $30,000 a month and expenses at $32,732. Of course, it would have been worse had they been totally honest about their expenses. The fact that they were losing money hadn't shocked them, but they hadn't realized how bad it was.

"So, what expenses can we cut?" I asked them at our next meeting?"

Don looked at the budget and then at Louise. "I guess we could cut one employee off of each shift. Everyone will have to work a little harder, but if that's what it takes for them to keep their jobs, I don't think they will complain."

"How much will that save?" I asked.

"About $1,500 a month."

"Good. That's half your deficit. How much are you two taking out of the business," I asked.

"A thousand a week each?" Louise replied.

"Well, since you won't have any credit card debt or car payments can you cut that a bit?" I asked.

Don nodded. "I suppose we could cut it back to $750 a week."

"Good. That puts us at about a break even. Now we need enough profit to pay our plan payments."

"How do we figure our plan payments?" Louise asked.

"Add up everything that must be paid in the plan, increase it by ten percent for the trustee's fee and divide that by sixty. I wrote down the numbers on a legal pad and added them up on my calculator.

"Okay, so if we add up all your debt it comes to $117,400. So after multiplying that by ten percent and dividing it by sixty, it looks like you will need to generate at least $2,152.33 profit each month. That will mean you will have to generate about an extra two thousand a month income or cut your expenses another $2,000. Of course, you'll have to pay interest on your secured debts so these numbers will vary somewhat but I think you get the idea."

"Right. I can see how it might work," Don said.

"One drawback of Chapter 13 or Chapter 11 is that there are a lot of rules and guidelines that you must adhere to while reorganizing. You can't borrow money or sell property without first giving notice to creditors and sometimes getting a court approval. You must keep all your post-petition debts current, pay all taxes in a timely manner and keep all of your property insured. These are all good rules but sometimes difficult to follow."

Two weeks later Don and Louise filed a chapter 13 bankruptcy and the automatic stay immediately took effect. They were elated when the notices went out and creditors quit calling. With the stress suddenly gone they were able to better focus on actually running the business and implementing the budget cutting that would be necessary to make their chapter 13 plan work. This was critical as the next step in the chapter 13 process was to convince the standing chapter 13 that the plan complied with the requirements of the bankruptcy code and was feasible.

The creditors meeting required under §341 of the Bankruptcy Code was set about a month later. After about a ten minute wait we were called in for our meeting that was to be conducted by Russell Burns, the business expert, from the Trustee's staff. Business cases required a higher degree of expertise so the Chapter 13 Trustee had an expert on the staff just to review business cases. After examining Don and Louise's driver's license and social security cards, they were sworn in and the meeting got under way.

"So, I'll need to see your profit and loss statement for the last six months," Mr. Burns said.

Don searched through a stack of papers he had brought with him and handed Mr. Burns the relevant documents."

He began studying them in earnest while we held our breath. After a few moments he looked up and shook his head. "It looks like we might have a feasibility issue. How do you propose to fund a plan when you're losing nearly $3,000 a month?"

"Ah. . . . Well, we've been working on reducing our expenses," Don said.

"Yeah. I realized that could be a problem when they first came in, so I had them rethink their budget. The numbers on Schedule I should be realistic."

Schedule "I" was where the debtors' personal and business budgets were located. Budgets were often times speculative at best so the trustee relied more on past history than a debtor's most optimistic view of the future.

"Well, you'll need to file a monthly profit and loss statement and we'll see how realistic your budget is. If I see you're not able to pay your bills as they come do I'll have to file a motion to dismiss the case or convert to Chapter 7."

Don squirmed nervously in his seat. Louise looked at me anxiously.

"We understand," I replied, "but I don't think that will be necessary. They understand how important keeping within their budget will be."

"Our sales are up ten percent, too," Don interjected.

The trustee nodded. "Good. I hope it all works out for you," he said and then proceeded to ask them a long list of routine questions to make sure they were in compliance with the bankruptcy code and understood all the rules they had to follow. When he was done he concluded the meeting.

Over the next few months Don and Louise continued to make the necessary adjustments to their budget and they soon were operating at a profit. Protected from creditors by the automatic stay, they were able to do more advertising and began contacting the people on their customer list trying to get them to come back. Many of them hadn't patronized their business in over a year thinking they'd gone out of business. As the profits soon exceeded their budget projections, Louise doubled up on their Chapter 13 plan payments and ended up paying the plan off in 36 months rather than 60.

Several years out of bankruptcy the Parkers were still doing well. In fact, they had expanded their operations adding another plant and two pickup stations. The landlord dropped the lawsuit over the roof and did not file a proof of claim for the cost of the repair to the roof. Apparently, all the insurance companies got together and worked it all out between them.

Case Study 2
Holiday Market

Back in the 1980s when there were still a lot of independent food stores around I had a client who operated half a dozen of them in the Dallas metroplex. He had acquired them from a chain store operation that had gone out of business. George Snyder was an accomplished grocer, having worked for a major chain store for over twenty years. He knew what he was doing and was often consulted by others operating retail grocery stores. In the past he had been the president of a major grocery trade organization.

At first the Holiday Markets flourished, and he was beginning to accumulate a nice estate. In fact, he first called me to do some estate and business planning. Like many entrepreneurs, he had been so busy operating his business, he hadn't taken the time to do the basic estate planning that every entrepreneur owner needs to do.

Unlike the average citizen who accumulates very few non-exempt assets in their lifetime, an entrepreneur will often create a valuable estate, sometimes worth millions. Of course, anyone with money becomes a target of promoters, aggressive businessmen, and outright scam artists out to relieve the entrepreneur of his money. Since George fit into this category, I recommended a defensive estate plan which also would minimize his estate tax liability. After we had buried his assets beneath layers of trusts, limited partnerships, and LLCs, I didn't hear from him for a while. Then one day George called and asked if I could come to see him.

Attorneys don't usually make house calls, but occasionally I'll have clients who expect me to come to them. I guess it's a question of whose time is more valuable. If a client thinks his time is more valuable than mine, and is willing to pay me to travel to him, I don't usually complain.

George's office was in east Ft. Worth off I-35E. George and his partner Hank Smith were both smokers so I nearly chocked when I entered his office. Fortunately, I had never been a smoker. Coughing, choking to death and setting myself on fire had never appealed to me, but I had learned to tolerate others who did it. George motioned for me to take a seat in the vacant side chair next to Hank.

"Thanks for coming by," George said soberly.

"No problem," I assured him. "What's the situation?"

Hank sat forward. "We're losing our shirt. That's the situation."

"Oh. Sorry about that. This economy has hurt a lot of people?"

"It's not only that," George said. "Usually the grocery business is resistant to recession. People have to eat, right?"

"I would think so," I agreed.

"It's the neighborhoods we're in. They've been declining a little year by year and now it's to the point sales just aren't enough to cover expenses."

"It's the Walmarts, Albertsons, and Krogers

springing up, everywhere too," Hank interjected. "It's hard to compete with them."

"So, what's your debt situation looking like?"

"We're running 45 days late on payables but our immediate problem is our money order payment."

"Oh, really. How does that work?"

"Well, we cash a lot of checks and get a fee for doing it. Once a week we're supposed to remit the cash to the money order company. The problem is we're supposed to make a $45,000 payment tomorrow but we don't have it."

"How come? Don't you keep that money segregated?"

"We're supposed to but we've just been putting the money into the operating account, you know, so we can take advantage of the float."

The float George was referring to was the time from the date money was deposited to when the check to the money order company cleared. If you consider the mail and normal turnaround time for the check that could be ten days to two weeks. During that time the $45,000 could be borrowed and used in the business. The problem was paying the money back once you had borrowed it.

"So, how did you expect to cover the check," I asked warily.

George sighed and Hank looked away, his face flushed. "Ah, well we usually get a coupon check twice a month," George explained. "That's the money to reimburse us for all the manufacturer's coupons we honor everyday. Unfortunately, Hank forgot to turn in the report last month!"

"Oh, I see. So, when will the coupon check be coming."

"I turned in the report yesterday, so we'll have it in two weeks."

"Hmm. So, have you ever been late paying the money order company?" I asked.

"No. And we won't be late this time either, but when they go to cash the check it's going to bounce!"

"Oh, God," I said, wondering how I could possibly extricate them from the mess they'd gotten themselves into. "Well, is there anyone who can loan you some money for two weeks until the coupon check clears?"

George shrugged. "I don't know who. I've exhausted all of my personal funds including my IRA."

"I'd loan the money to company," Hank said, "but my wife just filed for divorce and all my assets are frozen.

I sighed. "Well, you could file a Chapter 11 immediately. That would stop your creditors dead in their tracks, including the money order company."

"What about the check?"

"You'll have to stop payment on it and claim it would have been a preference to let it go through."

"Do you think they'll go for that?"

"Not for long, but it will buy you time and avoid the problem of the check bouncing for lack of funds. Since they didn't require you to segregate the funds and don't have a perfected security interest over any of your assets, they may just be an unsecured creditor. Hopefully, should they eventually be able prove the $45,000 wasn't part of the estate and belonged to them, by then you'll have the money to give them."

"God. I hate to do that," George moaned glaring at

Hank.

"I know," but if the check bounces and you're not protected by the automatic stay, no telling what will happen. I think this is your best shot."

"I don't know what we'll do if we can't sell money orders. Customers will stop cashing checks and a great deal of revenue will be lost—not only the check cashing and money order revenue, but all the sales that flow from the check cashing-customers."

I nodded. "Well, maybe you can find another money order company. If so, you can keep the funds in a separate account, so there is no question the money belongs to them. They will be protected, too since post-petition claims will have to be paid in a timely manner. If your Chapter 11 is not successful they will have a priority claim."

"I doubt anyone will touch us," George said.

"Oh, you never know. Your other option is to just shut down the business."

"I don't want to do that," George said.

George was a fighter and was determined to stay in business. As we continued to talk he explained to me how sales had slumped, he had cut overhead, increased advertising and consolidated operations between all his stores. But no matter what he did his operating capital continued to shrink until he was having severe cash flow problems.

George was a proud man, and I could tell having me there to discuss their perilous financial situation was killing him. After a while the smoke in his office was so thick that I got a terrible headache and could hardly think. It was time to go.

"Give it some thought," I said. "And let me know what you want to do."

After several days of discussions and planning, they agreed the only alternative was to file a Chapter 11. Of the six stores, only two were profitable, so the company was losing $20,000 a month. It was clear a reorganization was necessary even if the money order crisis had happened.

After the plan was filed, the U.S. Trustee's office called us in for the initial conference. They are charged with the oversight of Chapter 11 cases, so they bring in the debtor early on to make sure they know the rules of operating in Chapter 11 and are following them. One of the first things a debtor-in-possession, as Chapter 11 debtors are called, must do is shut down the old bank accounts and open new ones. These new debtor-in-possession accounts are set up to be monitored by the U.S. Trustee's office. Monthly operating reports must be provided to the court and trustee's office so they can track the debtor-in-possession's compliance with the intricate Chapter 11 rules of operation.

Several weeks later, the trustee conducted a creditors meeting, at which time creditors and the trustee asked questions of my clients and discussed the reorganization plan. The plan that we proposed was to sell the assets of the four unprofitable stores and use that money to pay off secured debts. The unsecured creditors would be paid 25% of their debt, thus putting the company in a position that it could be profitable in the future. In Chapter 11 a debtor can affirm or reject leases. This allowed Holiday Market to get out of its leases in the four unprofitable stores so that the company could concentrate on the two profitable ones.

Although in the bigger Chapter 11 cases a creditor's committee is usually appointed to represent all the unsecured creditors, often in smaller cases there aren't enough active unsecured creditors to have such a committee. This was the case with the Holiday Markets, and this made it easier to get our plan confirmed.

Once we had proposed a plan we put together a very comprehensive disclosure statement that explained the bankruptcy process to the creditors and gave them all the information about Holiday Market and its plan of reorganization such that they could vote intelligently when the plan was later put to a vote.

The plan was eventually approved by the creditors and confirmed by the court. It was a long, expensive process, but in the end was well worth the effort. We got the money order company to approve the plan by listing their debt as a priority class based on the theory that the money from sale of money orders didn't belong to the estate. Nobody objected to that treatment so they got all their money back over a five year period without interest.

A year later one of the remaining two stores was doing very well, but the other was still struggling. George had shut down his administrative office in Ft. Worth and set up shop at the West Dallas store. The downtown Dallas store was turned over to a manager who turned out to be incompetent. Unfortunately, George didn't realize it until it was too late. George's son took it over and tried to turn it around but the neighborhood was decaying and it was a losing proposition. Eventually that store had to be sold but not before I got a frantic call from Jeb, George's son.

"Jeb. What's up."

"We were just robbed!"

"Oh, no! What happened?"

"A man came in and went straight for the magazines. I didn't pay much attention to him as a lot of people like to do that—read the magazine on the shelf so you don't have to pay for it. But after a while I realized he'd been there over a half hour, so I called over to him to suggest he might want to go to the library. As soon as I said that he pulled a gun and came over to the register and told me to give him everything that was in it."

"Oh, my God." I exclaimed.

"So, I didn't have much choice but to give him everything in the registered since he had the drop on me. But, just as soon as he'd left the store I pulled out my .38 revolver and chased after him. I caught up to him just as he was getting into his pickup truck and fired two rounds. The first round missed him but the other one pieced a lung and brought him down. Unfortunately, one of our customers was in the line of fire and took the first bullet in her stomach."

My mind began to race as I considered the ramifications of what had just happened. Jeb could be charged with murder since the robber had died on his way to the hospital. He could argue that he was justified in going after the robber and shooting at him since he'd just robbed the store. On the other hand once the robber left the store there was no longer any risk of bodily harm to Jeb so he may not have been justified in going after him and killing him. The next problem was the spectator. If the customer died there could be a wrongful death suit without a doubt.

"Well, it's a good thing we did that defensive estate plan for your dad. At least his assets are tucked away where it won't be easy for anybody to take them away from you."

"Yeah, what little assets are left," George snickered.

"So, what did the police say?"

"The first officer on the scene said he didn't think the grand jury would indict me, but that they would have to consider it. They said I'd know in a few days."

The officer was right. The grand jury no-billed Jeb on the shooting of the robber. Unfortunately, the administrator of the spectator's estate sued Jeb, George and the LLC for wrongful death and got a judgment of $750,000. It didn't do them any good, however, as there were no non-exempt assets or unpledged assets laying around from which to collect the judgment.

Five years later, George retired and his son took over the last Holiday Market. The store was highly profitable for another ten years until it was destroyed one night by a raging fire. It was never rebuilt, as Jeb feared he would never be able to get their customers back after being out of business for several months.

With the insurance money and proceeds of the sale of the land upon which the store had been built, Jeb was able to buy two trucks and set up a short run trucking business which he successfully operates today.

Case Study 3
Tj Handbag & Belt

Sometimes for one reason or another a client refuses to file bankruptcy even though it seems to be the best way out of their financial distress. Once such case was T.J. Shah. TJ had owned a handbag and belt manufacturing plant in Euless, Texas for many years and had done very well. He owned a very expensive home, the land and building in which he operated his business, and had plenty of cash. Unfortunately he had only one major customer, a large department store chain.

In the mid-90s his department store customer began to struggle and had to close many of its stores. As a result, the big orders for purses and belts that he had grown dependent upon dropped drastically. The retail market at the time was bad, so TJ had difficulty replacing the declining purchases from this big customer. Eventually the department store owners filed Chapter 11 and receivables in excess of $100,000 had to be written off.

When TJ came to see me he was desperate. The IRS had garnished his bank accounts, there were several lawsuits in progress, and he was getting dozens of calls each day from creditors wanting to get paid. This was an obvious situation that called for a Chapter 11, but TJ, for personal and religious reasons, wouldn't hear of it.

Prior to coming to see me, he had managed to get

most of his creditors to accept payouts for what was owed them. He didn't like to pay attorneys, but needed me to defend a couple lawsuits that had been filed against him. The one that was most troublesome was from his biggest supplier who was owed $85,000. They were unsympathetic to TJ's financial situation and pressed hard for a judgment. After several months of bitter fighting, legal fees started to become a problem for TJ, and I wondered if he was going to make it. It seemed this adversary was intentionally invoking every legal maneuver in order to run up his legal bill.

TJ's biggest problem in reorganizing was getting supplies, as all his vendors had put him on a cash-only basis. He had to have raw materials to manufacture his goods, or he wouldn't have had anything to sell. But his cash was being drained by all the installment payout arrangements he had worked out with his creditors. To preserve precious cash, he had let all but his most critical employees go and was handling sales himself. Eventually, we got his lawsuits settled and his future seemed brighter. Business picked up and he was able to get a small line of credit from a new supplier. It seemed the worst was over.

TJ owed me quite a bit of money by the time I was through defending him, and I knew it would be a long time before I got paid, if at all. I didn't want to press him because of everything he had gone through already, so I just forgot about the bill. A year later out of the blue he called and said he had paid off several of the payouts and was ready to start working on my bill. I was shocked but thanked him for not forgetting about me. A day or two later he sent me 24 post-dated checks, which totaled the amount of my bill. He said to deposit one each month.

Now TJ is back on top and business is good. His customers are more diversified now, so he shouldn't be as vulnerable to a major drop in sales. All his old creditors have been paid and he is starting to put a little money away for the next avalanche or hurricane that strikes. TJ was able to weather the storm because he owned his own building, couldn't be evicted, and he was able to cut his overhead to a bare minimum until business picked up. Most importantly, he was determined to survive and never lost heart.

Case Study 4
Ztech, Inc.

Entrepreneurs often put their life savings into a new business venture even though they know their future will likely be very bleak if the business fails. This is not unusual. But when Austin Miles set up his new internet marketing company, he not only took out a home equity loan for $100,000, but also borrowed $250,000 from his father-in-law and $150,000 from his two best friends. His plan was to get the company off to a big start and then go public.

When he came to see me it wasn't because the new company wasn't doing well. In fact, it was performing beyond expectations. But, Austin had underestimated the time it would take to cash in on his stock options that were awarded to him when it went public. Under federal securities law he couldn't sell any of his shares for two years.

Although he was paid a nice salary it wasn't enough to cover the expected lifestyle of a corporate CEO. Consequently, with another year before he could cash in on his stock, his mortgage was in default, he couldn't pay his property taxes and his two friends were demanding payment of their notes.

Austin was a gregarious man in his mid-fifties, who always greeted you with a big smile. I liked him immediately and understood why he was a CEO. His charm, enthusiasm and optimism easily assuaged any concerns his colleagues or customers might have about whatever goods or ideas he was selling. After he sat down across from me one afternoon, he explained how he and a few friends had heard about a man who had developed some highly advanced robotic technology and they had partnered with him to form a new company, ZTech, Inc.

"So, the public offering went very well and my stock options are worth about 1.7 million today."

"Wow. That's a nice little windfall."

"Well, it was earned, believe me. You don't know what we went through to put it together."

"Right. I can only imagine."

"Our legal counsel for the offering also represented the President in another matter, so I have complete confidence the shares will double or triple in value over the next few years.

"The President?"

"Yes. George Bush."

Realistically, ZTech's legal counsel wouldn't have much to do with the fortunes of the start-up tech company, but I just nodded and raised my eyebrows trying to appear impressed, and said, "Oh, really?"

"Yes, so I just need to figure out a way to survive another year or so."

"Okay, so what problems are you facing now?" I asked, knowing there would be many and none of them simple.

"Well, I'm behind on my house payments?"

"How far behind?"

"My payments are $4,200 or so a month and I'm

about six months behind. So, about $25,000."

"Have you got a foreclosure notice yet?"

"No. They have been working with me, but I fear their patience is wearing out."

"So, have they threatened to accelerate the note?"

"Yes, I got a 30-day notice to catch up or they would accelerate."

"Okay. What else?"

"Ah, well . . . I owe about $28,000 in property taxes and the county has filed suit."

"Alright," I replied. "Keep going."

"Ah . . . then there are a couple of notes that are due to friends, say $150,000. My car payments are three months behind and I have about $165,000 in credit card debt."

I took a deep breath. "So, is that it?"

Austin shook his head. "I think so. Pretty much."

"So, your plan is catch up everything by cashing in your stock options."

He smiled broadly. "Yes, I'll have plenty to take care of everybody."

"How much income to do you receive now?"

"Well, the company is paying me $150,000 right now. I should get a raise to $200,000 next year."

"So, after you pay your bills each month, how much do you have left over?"

"Nothing!" I'm coming up short each month.

I forced a smile. "Well, you can't do a regular Chapter 7 bankruptcy unless you are willing to give up your stock options."

"No. No way! That's my only salvation. Once the restrictions come off my stock everything will be fine."

"Right. So, a Chapter 13 or 11 is about your only way out of this predicament."

"Okay. So, how will that work?"

"Well, in a Chapter 13 you could keep your stock options if you were willing to do a 100% plan."

"What does that mean?"

"It means everybody would have to get 100% of what was owed them in order for the plan to be confirmed."

"That's okay. I want to pay everyone everything."

"Good. The only problem is you may have too much unsecured debt to qualify for a Chapter 13. I think the limit is about $350,000."

Austin frowned. "Well, I owe way more than that."

"Right. That's too bad. A Chapter 13 would be a much better for you. It's much simpler, less dangerous and costs a lot less."

"What do you mean, dangerous?"

"A Chapter 13 is very routine. A Chapter 13 Trustee administers your plan, so it's not likely anyone would challenge you. And since it's a kind of cookie cutter operation the fee is quite modest, only $3,500."

"What's the alternative?" Austin asked.

"A Chapter 11. You would be what is called a debtor-in-possession. That would mean you would administer your bankruptcy yourself. We would have to develop a unique plan of reorganization and get it approved by the United States Trustee, a majority of your creditors, and the Judge assigned to your case."

"Okay. Is that hard to do?"

"It's not an easy task, so instead of $3,500 in attorney fees you would be looking at $10-20,000."

"Well, I don't have that kind of cash available."

"Most attorneys would insist on getting it all up front because, to be honest with you, most Chapter 11's are not successful. But, since you want to pay 100% to your creditors that should make it much easier to sell to them and the U.S. Trustee. So, if you can come up with $10,000, I could handle it for you."

"Okay. I'll come up with it somehow."

A few weeks later Austin came up with his $10,000 retainer and I got to work on his petition and schedules. In any bankruptcy the first task is to complete the bankruptcy petition, schedules, statement of financial affairs and other documentation required by the Bankruptcy Code. The information provided must be accurate and complete so a lot of time and effort goes into gathering the information required and filling them out. Some attorneys immediately file the petition to get the automatic stay in place and then file the schedules and other documentation later. This is dangerous for two reasons. Without gathering all the information for the bankruptcy ahead of filing, you don't know all the facts about your client and his affairs. It may turn out later when all the facts are in that the bankruptcy was a mistake. The other reason is you may not be able to gather all the information needed before the deadline for filing your schedules is upon you. If that happens your case may get dismissed. Either of these problems can be devastating.

Once the paperwork was complete I went down to the Federal Courthouse in Dallas and filed the case. Today, everything is done online so it's much easier that it was then. Since every Chapter 11 debtor-in-possession had to meet with the attorney assigned by the U.S. Trustee to manage the case, I called and got that meeting set up. Chapter 11s are complicated and governed by strict rules and guidelines so the U.S. Trustee required these meetings to make sure each case got off to a good start. It was also a good time for me to size up the attorney who I would have to convince to approve Austin's final Chapter 11 Plan. A week later Austin and his wife met me at the Courthouse and we went up to the U.S. Trustee's office on the 9th floor. Since Texas is a community property state, Austin's wife had to be included in the bankruptcy. After waiting five minutes in the reception area we were escorted to a conference room and told to wait.

Austin didn't seem to be the least bit concerned about the meeting but his wife, Shannon, looked anxious. I supposed as a corporate CEO he had meetings like this every day but his wife didn't. Several minutes later a middle-aged woman with dark hair walked in. She smiled and took a seat across from us. She identified herself as Sharon Simpson and indicated she had been assigned to monitor our case. After making us sign in, she explained what her role would be, her expectations of us and then began asking questions.

"So, have you set up your debtor-in-possession accounts?"

Chapter 11 debtors-in-possession had to close all of their bank accounts upon filing and open a new account at an approved bank.

"Not yet," I replied, "but we plan to do that right away."

"Be sure you do," she advised and handed Austin

a packet of papers. "Here is a list of approved institutions and the rules for operating the account."

Austin took the packet and started leafing through it.

"So, tell me about your business?" Sharon said.

Austin smiled and began telling her his story. Although he was very articulate and charming, Sharon showed no emotion throughout the presentation. I guessed she'd heard a lot of similar tales.

When he was done she turned to me and asked, "So, do you know what your plan is going to look like yet?"

"Yes. The Austins want to pay everyone they owe 100% but they need to do it over three years since Mr. Austin's ZTech stock can't be sold for another year or so. In the meantime, they will pay all current expenses as they come due and dedicate anything left over to pay arrearages on their secured debt, namely their home, automobiles, and property taxes.

"Once the restrictions on the ZTech stock are lifted then enough stock will be sold to pay any remaining debt."

"Well, that's admirable but you're betting on the stock remaining stable or increasing in price for the next two years."

"Yes," I agreed.

Sharon nodded. "Well, you know that's a gamble, right?"

I nodded. Sharon turned to Austin. "Mr. Miles. Have you been involved in startup companies in the past?"

"Sure," Austin replied. "I have been involved in

several of them."

"Have they all been successful?"

Austin frowned. "Well, not all of them."

"In fact, one of them has failed miserably and is no longer in business, isn't that right?"

Austin took a deep breath. "That's true, but another one was acquired by a competitor at a nice premium."

"I know. I just wanted to warm you that I am familiar with public offerings and if I see anything I don't like with your individual case or ZTech's stock performance, I won't hesitate to ask the court to dismiss the case or convert it to Chapter 7."

"That's understood," I interjected. "The Miles are fully committed to making their plan work, but if something unforeseen happens we will inform you immediately."

"Good," Sharon said and handed Austin another packet of papers. "Now, even though you are not personally in business, we still will need monthly financial statements. Will you be hiring an accountant?"

"No. I can fill out the forms," Shannon said. "I am a bookkeeper."

"Okay. Good. Reports are due on the 20th of each month. You will find instructions in your packet but if you still have questions feel free to call me."

"Thank you," Shannon said. "How do I file them?"

"Just deliver them here and have your attorney file a copy with the Court."

"Okay, thanks."

"That's all I have. Unless you have questions, we will adjourn and see all of you at the 341 Meeting."

The 341 Meeting refers to the meeting where creditors can come and ask the debtor-in-possession or trustee questions about the case, their claim or any other relevant issue. In small Chapter 11 cases there may only be a handful of creditors who show up at these meetings and they are usually secured creditors. If enough unsecured creditors show up and agree to participate, the trustee can appoint a creditors committee that will look out for the interest of all the unsecured creditors. I was hoping that wouldn't happen as it would complicate matters and make my job more difficult. I noted the date of the 341 meeting on my yellow pad and then stood up. We said our goodbye's and left.

While we were waiting for the elevator Austin asked, "So, how do you think that went?"

I shrugged. "Not bad. Ms. Simpson seems pretty reasonable. Since you are proposing a 100% plan her only real concern should be feasibility. Most debtors-in-possession only offer a 10-25% payment to unsecured creditors, so there is good reason for her to support us and help get your case confirmed."

"Good. So, what's next," Austin asked.

"Don't pay any bills or write any checks out of your old bank accounts. You need to shut them down. Tomorrow, we can go to the bank and set up your DIP account."

"DIP?" Shannon said.

"Yes, the Debtor-in-Possession account. You will both need to be there to sign the account agreement and signature cards."

"Okay, so that's it?" Austin asked.

"Yes, pretty much. Be sure and pay the current

mortgage, car payments and your regular bills on time. You can't get behind any further than you are."

"Okay."

"Over the next few months I will be working on your plan or reorganization and disclosure document."

"What's a disclosure document?" Shannon asked.

"It's a fairly extensive and complex document that explains the bankruptcy process, your Chapter 11 Plan, the approval process by creditors and the Court, and the risks associated with the plan. I will put a first draft together and then call you to set up a meeting to go through it and make any additions or corrections to it. We have four months to get it filed. Then it will take another couple of months to get it approved. In the meantime, enjoy the calm before the storm. Once it is approved the Court will schedule a confirmation hearing and if there is any opposition to our plan, that is when it will get resolved one way or another."

"What are our chances?" Austin asked.

"Good. Like I said, a 100% plan is pretty much a no-brainer for your creditors."

Much to my delight, there were only two creditors at the 341 meeting. A representative from the mortgage lender and one of Austin's friends who had an unsecured debt of $75,000. Since one unsecured creditor wasn't enough for an unsecured creditors committee, Sharon indicated on the record that she would not be setting one up. So far, everything had gone as expected and I was feeling good about the case, until Sharon closed the meeting and then talked to us off the record.

"I have one concern about this case, and I know it is one the Judge will have problem with as well."

"Okay. Sure, what is it?" I asked.

"Once the plan is approved everything depends on Mr. Miles exercising his options just as soon as the restrictions are lifted. I'm concerned that if Austin becomes incompetent or dies between the time the plan is confirmed and the date the options can be exercised, we'd have a problem."

"Right," I agreed. "So, what do you suggest?"

"Perhaps you could find a third-party, a bank or individual trustee to hold the options with instructions to exercise them at the appropriate time."

"I don't know if that would work," Austin replied. "You can't just sell all of the stock at one time. If the CEO of the company dumps all his stock, that might scare investors and cause the stock to take a nosedive. No, the stock must be sold off slowly."

"Well, you will need to address that issue in your plan and satisfy us that you will be able to sell enough shares to satisfy the plan requirements without negatively impacting the price of the shares."

"Okay. These are good points. I know a bank that might agree to act as trustee. We will work it out, I'm sure," I assured her.

"Good. Then I'll be looking forward to seeing your first monthly financial report next week and your plan of reorganization when you file it."

"Yes, thank you," I said.

When we got in the elevator, I asked Austin if we were going to have a problem when he started exercising his stock options and selling his shares. He gave me one of his gleaming smiles. "Nah. The trading should be active enough that selling 5% per month won't impact its value that much. I couldn't sell any more than that, though.

When I got back to my office I called a banker I had worked with on and an estate plan for a client. Reserve Bank had agreed to act as a trustee when the client revealed that he had no children or siblings to act as his executor and trustee should he die. Ted Small's professionalism and eagerness to help had impressed me, so I thought his bank would be perfect to handle the sale of Austin's stock and to distribute the proceeds to the creditors pursuant to the confirmed plan of reorganization. He listened to what I had to say and said he would look into it and get back to me. I prayed they would do it.

A few days later, Ted called me back and said not only would they do it, but if we let their securities department handle the transactions they wouldn't charge anything over their standard trading fees. That was good news and would save Austin a lot of money, so he agreed that was the way to handle it. After writing the first draft of the plan I prepared a spreadsheet to illustrate how it would work. Then I met with Austin and Shannon to go over the details of the plan and work through different scenarios using the spreadsheet. When we were satisfied the plan would work I addressed the issue of the disclosure document.

"Now, what could go wrong with this plan?" I asked. "We need to disclose every possible risk involved if this plan is implemented."

Austin and Shannon looked at each other and then Austin shrugged, I guess I could get fired. I only have a one year contract. The Board may not renew it if the company isn't performing as well as they would like."

"Would you lose your stock options?"

"No, but I'd lose my $200,000 salary, and I'm not sure how quickly I could get another job."

I nodded. "Okay, I'd say that is one of the risks that should be listed along with the possibility the stock price will fall."

"What about divorce?" Shannon asked.

Austin stiffened. "That won't happen."

"Hopefully not," I said, "but it is a risk even if you don't foresee it now."

Before we adjourned we had a list of over twenty-five things that could happen that would seriously jeopardize the plan of reorganization. Shannon was worried that nobody would vote for the plan after they read the risks involved, but Austin assured her that nobody paid any attention to disclosure statements.

"If they did," Austin said. "The stock market wouldn't exist."

I nodded my agreement having read a few disclosure agreements myself for clients and advising them to skip the investment. They rarely took my advice. A few weeks later, we filed the Plan of Reorganization and Disclosure Agreement and held out breaths. It was quiet for a few days, so I took that as a good sign and set a hearing on the adequacy of the Disclosure Document. That would be our first test along the road to getting our Plan of Reorganization approved.

Nobody objected to the Disclosure Document so it was routinely approved by the Court. The next step in the process was the vote by the creditors for or against the Plan. I didn't see how anyone could object to a 100%

plan, so I was optimistic. As the confirmation hearing approached nearly all of the ballots cast were in favor of the Plan, so I fully expected the Plan to be approved by the Court, but I was wrong.

After I had advised Judge Lamb that the Plan had been approved by each class of voters and asked that the Plan be confirmed, the judge turned to Sharon and asked, "What the United States Trustee's position on this Plan?"

Sharon cleared her throat and replied, "We support the Plan and urge the Court to confirm it."

The Judge gave Sharon a hard stare and then said, "Well, I have grave concerns about it. It's based on a lot of speculation and wishful thinking. It would probably be better for the unsecured creditors if the case was converted to Chapter 7 and an Interim Trustee be appointed to liquidate the stock."

"Your Honor," I objected. "The unsecured creditors have voted in favor of the Plan. They apparently believe it would be better if the Debtor-in-Possession sold the shares."

"They don't always know what's best for them. It's my responsibility to determine if the Plan is feasible and I don't see that as it is currently written."

"Your Honor, the Plan calls for a bank to liquidate the stock in accordance with the terms of the Plan. As soon as the Plan is confirmed, Mr. Austin will assign the stock option to the Reserve Bank who will liquidate it."

"I get that," the Judge said, "but you are gambling on the stock price remaining the same or increasing. I have seen a lot of these startup companies start off strong but quickly lose steam as time goes on."

"That risk was pointed out in the Disclosure Document," I reminded the Judge.

"I'm sorry, but I just can't confirm this Plan as it is currently written. I will continue this hearing for 30 days to give you a chance to amend the Plan to make it feasible."

I just looked at the Judge in disbelief, but there was nothing I could do, so I said, "Very good, Your Honor."

When I looked at Sharon she shrugged. I shook my head and turned to Austin. "Well, she didn't deny it, so there is still hope. Let me give what happened today some thought and I'll get with you later and figure out what to do next."

Dejected, Austin left to go home and tell Shannon what had happened. As I was leaving the Courtroom, an attorney I'd seen around but didn't know approached me. He smiled sympathetically and said, "Don't feel bad. This judge enjoys humiliating attorneys in front of their clients."

"Seriously," I said. "Is that what this was about?"

"Yes. I'm afraid so."

"So, what should I do?"

"I don't know. You should talk to one of his old law clerks. They might have some suggestions."

When I got back to the office, I checked online and found out the identity of the Judge's law clerks over the past few years. One of them, Gina Barrow, I'd met although I didn't know her that well. I dialed her number, told her secretary who I was and was put through. We chatted a moment and then I told her why I was calling.

"Yes, I saw the Judge unload on you in court. How can I help?"

"I'm at a loss as to what to do. I'm proposing a

100% plan, the creditors voted for it, the U.S. Trustee supports it but the judge doesn't think it's feasible."

"She's came to the bench from a securities firm, so she knows the underbelly of the securities business."

"Okay," I said. "So, what could I do to make the Plan more palatable to her?"

"If you hire me as co-counsel, I could redo your plan. Not that there is anything wrong with it, but Judge Lamb is very particular in how plans should be structured. The same goes with your disclosure document. It will be the same plan, just dressed differently."

"So, if we do that, you think we can get it confirmed."

"Yes. It shouldn't be a problem."

Austin didn't object to me bringing in co-counsel if it meant the Plan would be confirmed, so Gina amended the Plan and Disclosure Document and, as promised, got it confirmed at the continued hearing. The next step was to begin implementation of the Plan. After notifying the Bank that the plan had been confirmed, Austin arranged to have the options assigned to bank until they could be exercised. In the meantime, Austin began making the payments specified in the Plan.

For the next year I watched the stock price praying it would increase or at least stay the same. There were a few ups and downs, but overall the price hung around $19.00 per share. When it came time to start selling the shares, I held my breath that the first sale would not cause the stock to crash. As Austin promised the first sale didn't cause even a ripple in the stock's price. Over the next two years I felt better and better as Austin's creditors were gradually paid off. After the last stock was sold, the final payments made to creditors, and the case closed I felt great satisfaction that I had helped Austin and his wife keep their home and automobiles, pay their property taxes, pay off their credit cards, and pay their family and friends over a half million dollars.

After the case was over I quit watching the stock and had no further contact with Austin, but about a year later I got curious and looked up ZTech on the over-the-counter market. Much to my shock, the stock had nosedived and was trading for $1.11 per share! Further investigation led me to an article about how one of ZTech's competitors had developed a superior product and stole away many of ZTech's customers. I wondered if Austin had gotten out of ZTech before it crashed, but didn't call him to find out. Better I didn't know.

Ten Commandments for the Entrepreneur

1.I shall only pay myself from the profits of the business.

2. I shall keep accurate books and records so I will know how the business stands at all time.

3. I shall pay my taxes as they come due.

4. I shall avoid borrowing money and incurring unnecessary debt.

5. I shall treat my partners and employee's fairly and honestly.

6. I shall attend to each problem that confronts me and work hard until it is resolved.

7. I shall honor my attorney and pay him promptly.

8. I shall respect my insurance agent and buy insurance against the many risks that will confront me

9. I shall keep my overhead low and be ever mindful of ways to reduce operating costs.

10. I shall put aside a portion of my profits each year to help weather the storms that will inevitably come my way.

Conclusion

No matter how desperate your situation looks, if you take a deep breath and vow to take charge of your destiny, you can do it! You have the independent spirt, the drive, and the desire to be successful. Now you know the pitfalls to avoid and the tools you will need to be successful. It's time now for performance. No more excuses or whining about how you are a victim of the economy or the competition. You have achieved the American dream of owning your own business and being truly free. Don't let it slip out of your hands.

Obviously, if your small business is in dire straits, some sort of bankruptcy or reorganization will likely be needed to save it. I know this might be hard to swallow, but you're not a failure if you file bankruptcy. Congress enacted the bankruptcy laws to help people just like you to reorganize their businesses or get a fresh start. It's your right to take advantage of these laws to turn your business around. The reality is you may have to go broke to return your business to profitability and die rich.

It won't be easy. Nothing worthwhile ever is, but it will be the most fulfilling task you will ever perform. If you can turn your business around, and I know you can, you will feel an exhilaration few people have ever experienced. Your confidence will soar. Your health will improve, you'll feel younger, have more energy, and you will sleep soundly at night. But the best news is that your business will begin to flourish beyond your wildest expectations, as you have learned how to run a small business.

This isn't to say you won't ever have problems again. Obviously you will, but now that you are an astute entrepreneur, you will not be as dependent or controlled by your environment. With a lean, efficient operation you will sail through the recessions and the downturns by quickly adjusting to the marketplace. When times are good you won't loot your company but will set aside funds for future emergencies and pay off debts so that eventually you will be debt-free.

This isn't a dream or an idle fantasy. This can be your reality if you avoid the pitfalls I have pointed out to you, adopt the sound business practices outlined in this book and treat your employees and customers with courtesy and respect.

Good luck!

Glossary

Accountant - The number cruncher who all entrepreneurs desperately need to help them keep track of their money and keep the IRS off their back.

Accounting - The boring, tedious process of keeping track of your money so you know if you are making or losing it.

Attachment - a legal method available to judgment creditors allowing them to seize assets belonging to a judgment debtor.

Attorney - The greedy but streetwise SOB every business owner desperately needs in order to survive and thrive as an entrepreneur.

Automatic stay - a federal court order that takes effect immediately upon filing on a bankruptcy and stops creditors from taking any further action to collect the debts owed them by the debtor.

Board of directors - the group of men elected by the shareholders who are charged with the responsibility of operating the corporation between annual shareholder meetings. They typically elect officers to run the business on a day-to-day basis but make the important decisions.

Budget - An estimate of future income and expenses of the business over a period of time.

Business interruption insurance - Insurance that replaces lost revenue if the business is shut down for a period of time.

Buy-Sell Agreement - An agreement between shareholders or interest holders to buy the ownership interests of a retired, deceased or disabled owner.

Cash flow - The total amount of cash received by an entrepreneur from whatever source, less all expenditures for a given period.

CFO (Chief Financial Officer) - the person responsible for the financial well being of a business.

Collateral - property of the business that is pledged as security for the payment of a debt.

Competition - Other businesses in your neighborhood that provide goods or services similar to yours.

Confirmation - the process of approving a Chapter 11 or Chapter 13 reorganization plan.

Contract labor - Persons who work for more than one employer, part time or as needed, and are not under the direct control of the entrepreneur.

Constable - A law enforcement officer of a local government who often serves legal papers or tries to collect or enforce judgments of the civil courts.

Creditor's meeting - A meeting required in all bankruptcy proceedings, at which time the trustee and creditors can ask questions of the debtor. It is sometimes called a 341 meeting named after the bankruptcy code section from which it is authorized.

Debtor - A person or business entity that owes money to someone else; a person who has filed bankruptcy.

Debtor Adjustment - A Chapter 13 bankruptcy.

Debtor-in-possession - A person or business entity that has filed a Chapter 11 bankruptcy and remains in control of their business while it is reorganized.

Defensive estate plan - The structure of a person's financial affairs such that it is not vulnerable to sudden attack and loss to predators.

Disclosure Statement - a document required in a Chapter 11 case that provides the creditors with full disclosure of the Chapter 11 process, the history of the debtors, the terms of the proposed chapter 11 plan of reorganization, and the risks involved should the plan be confirmed.

Execution - The legal process by which a sheriff or constable attempts to collect a judgment from the judgment debtor.

Embezzlement - When a trusted employee or family member steals money from you a little at a time so it goes unnoticed.

Exempt property - The property, as provided by federal or state laws, which a debtor in bankruptcy can keep and won't lose after filing bankruptcy. Also, that property by state law that is protected from execution by judgment creditors.

Form 940 & 941 - Employment tax returns that must be filed each quarter by every business that has employees including owners and officers.

Form 1040 - The income tax form that must be filed each year by individuals and individual entrepreneurs.

Garnishment - A collection method available to judgment creditors that compels third parties to pay over money they owe to the judgement debtor to them instead.

General Partnership - A type of business relationship where individuals act together in a business venture sharing profits, losses and liabilities. It is generally not a preferred way to do business and should be avoided.

General Liability Insurance - Insurance that

protects a business from claims of persons injured by the acts of the business, its employees or owners.

Joint Venture - Another term for a general partnership which is a risky way to do business.

Judgment Creditor - A creditor who has obtained a judgment from a court of law fixing the amount owed to him by a debtor.

Judgment Debtor - A person or business entity that has a judgment rendered against them by a court of law, fixing the amount that is owed.

Loan consolidation - The process of paying off several small loans from the proceeds of a bigger loan, hopefully at a lower interest rate, payable over a longer term and with lower monthly payments.

Looting - The common practice of small business owners to suck every dollar they possibly can from their businesses to support their lavish lifestyles until the business can't support itself and goes under.

Member - One of the owners of a limited liability company, called an LLC, (like a shareholder of a corporation). The members usually run the LLC without of board of directors.

Non-recourse debt - A form of secured debt that, in the event of a default, the creditor will take the collateral in full satisfaction of the debt and not seek damages from the business or its owners.

Partners - The owners of a partnership whether it be a general partnership, limited partnership or joint venture.

Plan of Reorganization - The plan a debtor-in-possession files in a Chapter 11 bankruptcy proceeding.

Plan payment - The amount of money a debtor must pay each month to creditors in a Chapter 11 or

Chapter 13 bankruptcy.

Plastic - Credit cards

Post-Petition - The period of time after a bankruptcy is filed.

Predators - Greedy individuals and business entities that search out of ways take money away from honest, hard-working SBOs, and sometimes called "vultures."

Pre-petition - The period of time before a bankruptcy is filed.

Pro Se defendant - A defendant who answers a lawsuit himself without obtaining legal counsel—otherwise known as an "idiot."

Redemption Agreement - An agreement by the corporation to buy the shares of stock owned by a deceased or disabled shareholder.

SBO - Small business owner or entrepreneur

Standing Chapter 13 Trustee - The trustee who oversees and administers all chapter cases in a particular district.

Stockholders/shareholders - the owners of a corporation

Succession planning - Agreeing in advance what will happen if a partner, shareholder, or interest holder dies, divorces, becomes disabled or leaves the employment of the business.

Suffocation - The tendency of small businesses owners to have too much overhead, the cost of which will eventually put them out of business

Trustee - A person who is appointed by the U.S. Trustee's office to oversee a bankruptcy proceeding; a person who is appointed to handle a fund of money under a trust instrument

United States Trustee - the person who oversees all bankruptcies that are filed in a particular federal district.

Workmen's compensation - a form a insurance to protect a business from liability for employee's on the job injuries.

www.ingramcontent.com/pod-product-compliance
Lightning Source LLC
Chambersburg PA
CBHW050526190326
41458CB00045B/6716/J
9781733328326